100 YEARS OF FASHION

Cally Blackman

Laurence King Publishing

LAURENCE KING

Published in 2012 by
Laurence King Publishing Ltd
361–373 City Road
London EC1V 1LR

Tel: +44 20 7841 6900
Fax: +44 20 7841 6910

Email: enquiries@laurenceking.com
www.laurenceking.com

Reprinted 2012

© text 2012 Cally Blackman

This book was produced by Laurence King
Publishing Ltd, London

A catalogue record for this book is available
from the British Library.

ISBN-13: 978 1 8566 9 798 9

Designed by Praline: Guglielmo Rossi, David Tanguy

Printed in China

Front cover: © Norman Parkinson / Corbis

100 YEARS OF FASHION

Contents

1963 Jean Shrimpton in Marc Bohan for Dior

Introduction

This book shows fashion as it was represented in the ideal world and lived in the real world over the last century. This period witnessed the most rapid development in the production and dissemination of fashion to date, and the greatest transformation in its consumption: from the dominance of couture for the elite few at the turn of the twentieth century, to the near-universality of fast-fashion today, on the high street or at the click of a mouse. Catwalk shows are now streamed live on the internet; designer collections are assimilated by high-street chains almost overnight; fashion-forward looks on the street are relayed by a groundswell of digital media: affordable clothes are bought in quantity and discarded at will. This transformation in fashion's consumption reflects, and is inseparable from, the seismic changes in society that have taken place over the last century: the end of empires and colonial rule, revolutions fuelled by political ideologies, two World Wars, economic and environmental disasters, artistic movements, design innovation and the digital age; all have shaped the way we live now and the way we now live fashion.

The domination of the leading couture houses, dressmakers and tailoring establishments of Paris and London that held sway for a hundred years was challenged in the early twentieth century by the avant garde, who disdained bourgeois values: by the 1940s a sartorial revolution was gathering pace (in tandem with access to a wider variety of music) in the form of sub-cultural and youth-oriented styles that became immensely influential in the second half of the century. In the United States, clothes' manufacturing processes were streamlined and standardization of sizing pioneered, driving the ready-to-wear market, and new fashion democracies were forged in which reliance on the Old World was replaced by the homegrown talent of the New. The regeneration of haute couture after the Second World War lasted only a decade: by the 1960s, couturiers either responded to the youthful zeitgeist, or went out of business. Prêt-à-porter, diffusion lines and a focus on commercial franchises kept the couture industry afloat, making the designers more accessible, yet a continuing emphasis on luxury and exclusivity maintains the polarization between high fashion and the mainstream. Celebrity is the new aristocracy: a century ago the language communicated by clothes was easier to interpret, the sartorial codes given off by a duchess distinct from those imparted by a middle class housewife. These signs are now much more difficult to read: what we wear is no longer dictated by class, status or occupation, but is a reflection of money, aspiration and fame. Fashion, like society, is more fluid but not necessarily more democratic.

Fashion is frequently scorned as superficial, a result of its inbuilt ephemerality. As 'garment manufacture', it might be recognized more positively as the trillion-dollar global industry it is now, employing hundreds of thousands of people across the world to meet our ever-increasing demand for novelty and need for self-expression in the post-modern age. We are all subjects of fashion: as Oscar Wilde, with typical irony, said in *The Picture of Dorian Gray*: 'It is only the shallow people who do not judge by appearances'.

1901–1959

1901–1959

1907 Mlle Wilford in toilette de ville by Doucet *Les Modes*
A day dress for April with fur stole and feathered hat by Doucet, one of the oldest couture houses in Paris. Known for delicate, feminine designs that epitomized the Art Nouveau aesthetic, the house did not adapt to the sleek styles of the modern age, closing in 1932.

At the beginning of the twentieth century fashion was dictated by the Parisian couture houses, the most prestigious of which, founded in the mid nineteenth century by Englishman Charles Frederick Worth (1825–1895), continued to dress the top echelons of society: royalty, aristocracy, wealthy women, 'professional beauties' and celebrities of the day who peopled the fashionable world.

Those who could not afford the House of Worth's exorbitant prices patronized one of the many other couturiers, such as Doucet, Doeuillet, Laferrière, Jeanne Paquin or the Callot Soeurs. Appointed dressmakers in St. Petersburg and London provided court and ceremonial dress, while British firms such as Redfern, and Creed, both with Paris branches, were the acknowledged masters of the tailored garment, still an important element of female dress.

The cream of American society, those included in Mrs Astor's 'Four Hundred' (the number of guests that could fit into her New York ballroom), made frequent trips across the Atlantic to buy clothes: Astors, Cooper Hewitts, Morgans, Potter Palmers and Vanderbilts, among them the 'dollar princesses' who bolstered the fortunes of both the couture houses and the impoverished European aristocrats whom they married in return for title and rank.

Entire trousseaux were ordered for young brides, fabulous sums spent on toilettes ordered, sometimes by the dozen, to meet the demands of a hectic social life that required different clothes for different times of day and degrees of formality. Throughout the day – morning, riding, afternoon, visiting, relaxing *en famille*, dinner, evening, ball, gala, opera, theatre and court – all occasions demanded specific outfits, necessitating a minimum of three or four changes. Mourning dictated a range of garments in black. Lavishly decorated with embroidery, beading, rare lace and tulle, accessorized with furs, these opulent ensembles were the ultimate statements of conspicuous consumption. The constricting S-bend corset that pushed the bosom forwards and the hips backwards; high, wired collars, a bosom draped in a froth of lace and chiffon, monumental picture hats decorated with flowers, feathers and sometimes whole birds, resulted in a heavy, statuesque at best, appearance.

High Society was ruled by the Season, in the early summer, a hectic round of social events: from the presentation of debutantes and the visiting *haut monde* at court – spectacular occasions that required the most formal dress and a full panoply of glittering jewels – to the races at Ascot, Chantilly and Cowes. These were interspersed with numerous receptions, dinners and balls. After the Season ended, summers were spent at villas in fashionable resorts such as Biarritz or Deauville, cruising the oceans on luxury yachts, shooting on Scottish estates or languishing at Long Island house parties, before returning to 'Town' for the autumn social round. Velvet, satin or silk evening gowns revealed bare shoulders and arms encased in long kid gloves and a generous décolletage on which to display jewellery. Daywear consisted of tailored suits or elaborately embellished gowns accompanied by a plethora of accessories, from picture hats to parasols. Simpler summer frocks or blouses and skirts made from cotton, lawn and linen were trimmed with broderie anglaise or lace. These extensive wardrobes included ensembles from Paris fashion houses, several of which had branches in New York and London, and also licensed copies of their couture models to be made by manufacturers and dressmakers. Accessories and lingerie were purchased from specialist houses, or the more exclusive department stores.

Some women chose not to conform to society's expectations, dressing 'artistically', outside mainstream fashion. These 'bohemians' moved in avant-garde circles and might buy from Liberty or the Omega Workshops in London, Fortuny in Venice, or the Wiener Werkstätte, a small but influential co-operative of artists and designers in Vienna that aimed to reform dress. Female artists, such as the painter Sonia Delaunay, embarked on a mission to integrate fashion and art, or to design clothes that expressed new ideologies – including the Russian Constructivists Liubov Popova and Vavara Stepanova. These women were part of the intense artistic experimentation taking place during the first two decades of the century. New 'isms' were burgeoning across Europe: Fauvism and Cubism in Paris; Secessionism in Austria; Expressionism in Germany; Futurism in Italy and Constructivism in Russia; to be followed by Surrealism and Modernism. Painters, poets, musicians, writers and architects inhabited a mythical land called Bohemia (whether in reality based in Bloomsbury, Montmartre or Schwabing) where dress was symbolic of freedom from bourgeois constraint, physical constraint and, more importantly, of their aim to integrate all aspects of art and design, including dress, into daily life: so-called *Gesamkunstwerk*, the total work of art. Diaghilev's Ballets Russes, their revolutionary music, stage sets and costumes, introduced a further dramatic influence on contemporary culture, including fashion, after their first sensational season in Paris in 1909.

In Paris, Paul Poiret (1879–1944), who opened his salon in 1903, was the first couturier to match this dynamism in his work, simplifying the silhouette, relying not on complex construction but dramatic colour schemes, combined with exquisite surface decoration, for effect. His early *Directoire* line was followed, around the turn of the decade, by an Orientalist mode: loose, wrapped kimono-style coats with Chinese, Japanese or Persian motifs, diaphanous tunics wired at the hem, edged with fur or gold fringing and worn over harem pants. The English-born Lucile (Lady Duff Gordon 1863–1935) was a successful designer whose delicate 'gowns of emotion', with suitably melodramatic names such as 'The Sighing Sound of Lips Unsatisfied', modelled by statuesque mannequins, were less daring than Poiret's but also influenced by artistic considerations.

Since the last quarter of the previous century, women had been admitted to some universities and the struggle for the vote was well under way, although universal suffrage in England was not won until after the First World War. The bicycle and public transport enabled independent travel for the masses; a greater variety of jobs became available and more women worked, although for many, domestic servitude or factory labour remained the only options. Women's lives were changing rapidly, a process accelerated by the outbreak of the First World War. Some went to the front as doctors, nurses, drivers, or members of the auxiliary forces; those who remained at home replaced men absent from factories, on transport and working the land. Several of these occupations required women to adopt the forms of dress traditionally the preserve of men: practical breeches, trousers or overalls.

c. 1929 Alma Smith sunbathing
Sun worship was encouraged by doctors and scientists as beneficial to health. Here Alma Smith, a soubrette in musical theatre, stands under a sun lamp to get her daily dose of ultraviolet.

The 1914–1918 war barely slowed the business of high fashion: many Parisian couturiers continued to show their collections, although the dangers of Atlantic crossings limited the attendance of foreign buyers, press coverage and exports to North America, where department stores seized the opportunity to fill the temporary vacuum by promoting American designers. However, the allure of French couture was too great to be overshadowed for any significant length of time and afterwards Paris regained its position as the capital of fashion. Some changes of sartorial necessity also reverted to prewar status – trousers were not accepted as fashionable dress for women for many years, only worn by a daring few until well after the Second World War. What had changed was society itself: the old social hierarchies began to disappear as a result of war, revolution, political upheaval and economic hardship: the days when wealthy households employed vast retinues of domestic staff were gone forever.

The New Woman of pre-War days became the Amazon of the Art Deco era, or the independent Flapper who cut her hair into a short bob, drank cocktails, possibly took drugs, certainly smoked in public and danced late into the night at fashionable clubs, cabarets or bohemian dives. The majority of women did not live like this, of course; the Flapper was more a figment of retrospective popular imagination than fact, although the media attention given to the scandalous behaviour of the 'Bright Young Things' might lead one to believe otherwise. The androgynous *garçonne* style of the 1920s flattened the bosom, dispelled the waist and revealed the legs, reducing the silhouette to a short tube, topped with head-hugging cloche hat. Corsets were not totally abandoned, but moderated to achieve the required boyish figure; the development of new materials, including elastics and zippers (patented in 1924) made foundation garments less cumbersome, while synthetic fibres such as rayon made hosiery and lingerie less expensive and more appealing. By the end of the 1920s, hemlines were wavering; handkerchief points or dipped hems marked the transition from Flapper to glamour and a figure-revealing, more feminine silhouette emerged in the 1930s.

Travel and transport were improving rapidly: women embraced the excitement of speed on the roads and the racing track, female aviators joined them as pioneers of the modern machine age. Initially, these Amazons wore protective clothing similar to that worn by men: leather jackets, overalls, helmets and goggles, or they adapted everyday dress as they did for sports such as tennis, skiing and golf. As the popularity of sport increased, dedicated sportswear became the speciality of some couture houses such as Jean Patou (1880–1936) and Elsa Schiaparelli. The stretch quality ideal for active wear was provided by knitted fabrics that also transformed swimwear from voluminous bathing dresses with bloomers to streamlined garments giving maximum exposure for tanned bodies and slim figures honed by new exercise crazes and dietary regimes: the athletic figure became an expression of modernity.

Four female couturières dominated Paris in the interwar years: Jeanne Lanvin, Madeleine Vionnet, Coco Chanel and Elsa Schiaparelli.

Jeanne Lanvin (1867–1946) was best known for her pretty, romantic *robes de style*, taffeta evening gowns with paniered skirts inspired by eighteenth- and nineteenth-century silhouettes. Her meticulous research into historical and ethnic dress and textiles informed her aesthetic approach

1931 Clara Bow in *No Limit*
Clara Bow became the original 'It Girl' when she starred in the film of the same name in 1927. In a shimmering silver lamé dress, possibly by Travis Banton (head costume designer at Paramount Studios 1925 – 1938), she exudes the glamour and sex appeal cinemagoers came to see.

c. 1935 Evening dress
Hollywood attracted female audiences through glamour. Cinemas ran newsreels of fashion shows and features on the world of couture that allowed a glimpse into the lives of the rich, famous and fashionable. A gold sequined evening dress shows the influence of Hollywood style.

and unwavering style. That she maintained her success during a period when this style bucked the current trend is testament to her skill in interpreting what many women actually wanted to wear.

Madeleine Vionnet (1876–1975) will always be associated with the bias cut, i.e. cutting fabric at a 45° angle rather than along the straight grain. She was not the first to use this method, but she explored it to its fullest potential by draping, knotting and twisting supple fabrics to highlight the contours of the body in much the same way as the Classical dress she studied on Greek vases. Her innovative construction methods dispensed with seams and fastenings, resulting in garments whose simple appearance belied their complexity.

Coco Chanel (1883–1971) was, in life as well as in her work, the great exponent of modernism in dress, designing clothes in fluid jersey fabrics, easy-to-wear separates derived from sportswear and men's garments. The best exemplar of her own style, she wore trousers on holiday, mixed costume jewellery with the real thing and made a suntan fashionable. She was the first designer to put her name on a perfume bottle with the launch of CHANEL Nº5 in 1921 and she lifted black from the colour of mourning to the failsafe colour of elegance with her 'little black dress' of 1926. Her signature tweed suits and two-tone shoes, still updated seasonally by Karl Lagerfeld, are instantly recognizable as the inventions of a woman who has been called the most influential designer of the twentieth century.

Elsa Schiaparelli (1890–1973), having been successful with a small range of knitwear, set up her fashion house in Paris in 1928 with a focus on playful but practical styles and sportswear that appealed to a broad range of clients, including Hollywood film stars. She became known for sharp, tailored suits, embellished with embroidery and beading with a twist of fantasy and wit, in the form of a lollipop button or a humorous buckle. She was always highly experimental but it was her collaborations with the Surrealists, including Salvador Dalí and Jean Cocteau, that broke new ground in the attempt to make fashion art and art fashion. This mission still continues, despite the inherent dislocation between the two, namely that fashion has to function.

By the early 1930s, the fashionable silhouette was evolving into a slender, elongated torso with widening shoulders and a neat head with softly waved short hair. Tailored suits and floral dresses were fitted at natural waist level and flared out to the hem. For evening, body-hugging satin gowns were given dramatic effect by being backless, worn with lavish fox furs, or short bolero jackets. This was a sophisticated look epitomized by Hollywood stars whose every outfit was avidly followed by thousands of adoring fans whether on screen, in the movie fanzines or general press. It was the 'Golden Age' of cinema, the single most popular form of entertainment between the Wars, attracting huge audiences on a weekly basis. Stars adhered to various stereotypes from Clara Bow's Flapper and Theda Bara's vamp, to Marlene Dietrich's *femme fatale* or Greta Garbo's exotic Mata Hari. The major studios employed their own in-house costume designers, Travis Banton and Edith Head at Paramount and Gilbert Adrian at MGM; Head and Adrian each went on to launch their own clothing lines.

Cinema was a major disseminator of fashion in the interwar period. Department stores opened sections dedicated to promoting film costumes and Hollywood claimed to have more influence over women's fashion choices than Paris couturiers, who in turn found they had little or no influence over Hollywood. Chanel and Schiaparelli were commissioned to design for the cinema, but failed to understand the need for timelessness: when the movies were eventually released, their clothes looked outdated. Hollywood costume designers did influence fashion, the runaway success of Adrian's dress for Letty Lynton (p. 142) being one example, but perhaps the most enduring influence of Hollywood was in the field of cosmetics. Every woman could imitate and buy into, at relatively little cost, the look of her favourite stars, if only through copying their makeup and hairstyles: cinema democratized the empire of fashion by making glamour accessible.

When the world was plunged into war a second time, in 1939, many women again went into uniform; on the home fronts people were expected to be thrifty, to recycle and to 'Make Do and Mend'. Clothing was rationed from 1941 in Britain and France and from 1942 in America with the introduction of the L-85 order. Rationing restricted the amount of clothing people could buy as well as the quantity and type of fabric that could be used. The Utility scheme, introduced in 1941 in Britain, ensured that garments and other goods were manufactured to a high standard. The Incorporated Society of London Fashion Designers (IncSoc), founded in 1942, was commissioned to design a range of clothes that demonstrated Utility clothing could be stylish while conforming to rationing restrictions. In France, following the Nazi Occupation, from 1940 shortages quickly became acute and the black market in clothing thrived. Some items escaped rationing: hats became vehicles of self-expression, especially in Paris, and in Italy shortages of materials encouraged innovation in shoe design. People adapted because they had no choice, but still went to great lengths to retain a sense of fashion.

Thanks to the efforts of couturier Lucien Lelong, President of the *Chambre Syndicale*, the governing body of couture, who managed to prevent Hitler's attempts to relocate the industry to Germany, Paris couture survived throughout the war with over one hundred houses remaining open. Some non-French designers such as Mainbocher returned home: Elsa Schiaparelli went to America and Coco Chanel closed her house and spent the war at the Ritz Hotel in Paris and subsequently ten years in exile in Switzerland. On her return to Paris in 1954 at the age of seventy, she continued to perfect her signature style, having all but missed the seismic changes in fashion brought about by Christian Dior's 'New Look' collection of 1947.

The New Look, a term coined by *Harper's Bazaar* fashion editor Carmel Snow, brought back feminine curves and many of the intricate and laborious methods used in making couture garments. Dior's lavish use of costly fabric was shocking to many of those who had endured years of rationing and his return to a nineteenth-century silhouette, achieved by complicated, internal structuring was seen as retrograde. And yet, most fashion-conscious women were enchanted by the escape from austerity and return to femininity, quickly altering their clothes to suit Dior's vision. For the next decade, the so-called 'Golden Age of Couture', buyers, editors and clients were in thrall to the Paris couturiers: Dior, Balenciaga, Jacques Fath, Balmain and Hubert de Givenchy, among others. Patterns were licensed by couturiers for cheaper manufacture – though often garments were copied outright, much to the chagrin of the houses, who tried to eliminate this practice with strict controls over access to their shows. High fashion dominated the high street as mainstream manufacturers slavishly interpreted each season's new couture styles at prices affordable for the majority of women.

Italy recovered quickly from the War, soon establishing a reputation for glamorous fashion publicized by the stars, local and international, of the

1945–46 Dress by Lucien Lelong
for *Théâtre de la Mode*
Lelong's spotted chiffon summer dress with
softly draped neckline and fullness at the
hips, emphasized by a sash bow, indicates
that the silhouette was changing before
the tipping point of 1947's New Look.

newly invigorated Italian movie industry based at the Cinecittà studios near
Rome. Collective shows were held in Florence from 1951; these subsequently
moved to Rome, which became the centre of Italian *alta moda*. London retained
its reputation for traditional fine tailoring and smart country wear. The social
whirl of the Season still generated a significant part of the London couturiers'
income and ensured they were also known for romantic evening dress and the
outfits designed for members of the Royal Family by couturiers such as Norman
Hartnell and Hardy Amies.

There were changes in the air that would challenge and finally defeat
the hegemony of couture in the second half of the twentieth century. American
buyers unable to visit the Paris shows during the war began to foreground
their own homegrown talent: the American press declared the end of Paris's
dictatorship; Mainbocher and Charles James both returned to New York and
were regarded as its most prestigious couturiers. But it was the ready-to-wear
designers such as Norman Norell, Hattie Carnegie and Claire McCardell,
among others, who finally established New York as a rival fashion capital
during this period, no longer subservient to Paris but different, making
streamlined, elegant clothes for modern women who had careers and families
to run: the 'American Look' was born.

It was also in America that the 'teenager' was first recognized by
sociologists as a separate social entity in her own right, an individual who
dressed according to the group she belonged to, rather than emulating the
older generation. Postwar baby boomers in America (less so in Europe, which
took longer to recover economically after the war) had money to spend on
clothes and consumer goods: American styles were disseminated by popular
angst-ridden teenage movies such as *Rebel Without a Cause* (1955) featuring
James Dean and Natalie Wood, and through the music of idols such as Benny
Goodman, Frank Sinatra, Elvis Presley and Buddy Holly, among others. The
style of American youth subcultures such as the Bobby-Soxers became the
inspiration for teenagers on the Continent: the Swing Kids, the Modernists,
Zazous, Teddy Girls and Beatniks, and these in turn began to influence
mainstream fashion: the first tremors of the 'Youthquake' of the 1960s were
already being felt.

High Society

'In the Paris of my youth there were
no motorcars.... The Rue de la Paix was
the fashionable shopping centre and
names of the great dressmakers – Worth,
Doucet, Rouff – were printed on small
doors admitting one to modest shops.
Inside, the array of lovely dresses,
expensive furs and diaphanous lingerie
fairly took one's breath away.'

Consuelo Vanderbilt Balsan: *The Glitter and the Gold* 1952

**1902 Consuelo, Duchess
of Marlborough**
The most famous 'Dollar Princess'
of all, Consuelo Vanderbilt, who became
9th Duchess of Marlborough during
a short first marriage, in crimson silk
velvet peeress's robes for the coronation
of Edward VII. The design of her coronet,
the amount of ermine on her robes
and the length of her train symbolize
her high rank. She prepared for the long
day in Westminster Abbey by filling
her pockets with chocolate.

1902 Queen Alexandra
The new Queen Consort to Edward VII
in her coronation robes. A gold tissue
dress woven in India is overlaid with
Parisian spangled and embroidered
net; a purple velvet mantle embroidered
with royal emblems is attached to her
shoulders under a gold lace, pearl-
embroidered ruff collar. A king's ransom
of jewels festoons her bosom and neck,
including five rows of diamonds worn as
a choker, a style she made fashionable
although in her case it was designed
to conceal a small scar.

1914 Czarina Alexandra Feodorovna
The doomed wife of Czar Nicholas II
in full Russian court dress. A heavily
embroidered gown with hanging sleeves
in the style of the previous century
is worn with fan, gloves and a lace veil
suspended from the Romanov pearl
kokoshnik-style tiara.

**c. 1900 Evening dress
by Nadejda Lamanova**
From the wardrobe of the last Czarina,
an evening dress of spangled and
silver-embroidered white tulle, chiffon,
brocade and lace over a satin
underdress designed by Nadejda
Lamanova, official dressmaker
to the Russian Imperial court. After the
revolution in 1917, Lamanova continued
designing and helped to set up the
Soviet design school VKhUTEMAS.

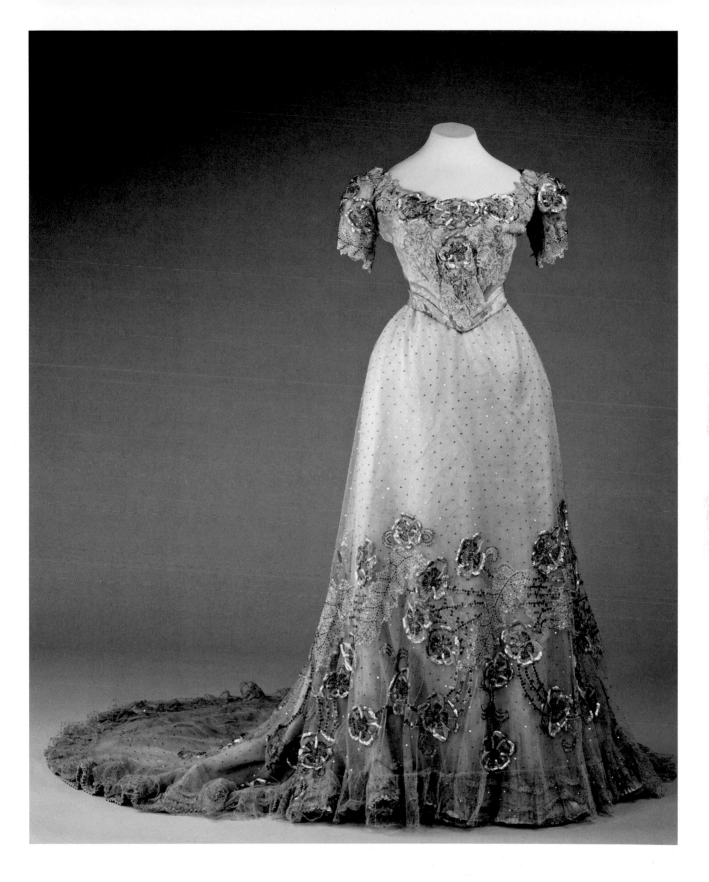

**1902 Formal evening gown
by Redfern, *Les Modes***
A robe *de Grande Cérémonie* 'as worn
at the English court' shown on the cover
of upscale French fashion magazine
Les Modes. This gown would have been
worn at the most formal court occasions,
held in the evening.

**1903 *Lady Mary Curzon*
by William Logsdail**
As Vicereine of Imperial India, American-
born Lady Mary Curzon represented
Queen Alexandra in spectacular fashion
at the second Coronation Durbar
in Delhi, in 1903. Her dress for the State
Ball, designed by Worth, was made
of cloth-of-gold, embroidered in India
with peacock feather motifs, each eye
studded with an emerald that glittered
in the newly installed electric light.

c. 1912 Queen Mary
The spectacular Cambridge and Delhi
Durbar parure, an emerald and diamond
tiara, choker, pendant and stomach
jewel made by Garrard the Crown
Jewellers for the 1911 Coronation Durbar
in India which she attended as Empress.
The Queen also wears the Garter Star
and, on her left arm, the Order of the
Garter. Since remodelled, the tiara
remains the property of the present
Queen and has been worn by the late
Diana Princess of Wales and the
Duchess of Cornwall.

1902 Gala dress by Maggy Rouff,
Les Modes
A less formal court or society occasion, such as a gala, required only slightly less formal dress. Here a gown by couturière Maggy Rouff displays a generous amount of décolletage but a relatively modest train.

c. 1905 Lady Lee and sister
Formal, trained evening dress was required for presentation at court, essential for anyone aspiring to join London high society. The wealthy American Moore sisters (Ruth became Lady Lee of Fareham and is possibly presenting her sister here) wear the regulation three white ostrich feathers, of the badge of the Prince of Wales, on their heads.

1922 Princess Shimazu of Japan
International dignitaries conformed
to regulations when presented at court:
the gown could change according
to current fashion, but train, feathers,
fan and gloves remained de rigueur.
Early morning sittings were held
at fashionable photographic studios
such as Lafayette to record the
occasion. The ostrich-feather fan has
now replaced the earlier bouquet.

1931 Wallis Simpson
The immaculately groomed future
Duchess of Windsor in her presentation
outfit, which she borrowed for the
occasion. A few years later, as the Prince
of Wales's mistress, she patronized
Parisian couturiers, becoming known as
one of the world's best-dressed women.

1910 Black Ascot
In June 1910, court and society
were still in mourning for Edward VII,
who had died in May, and dressed
accordingly at one of the main events
of the Season. 'Black Ascot', as it
became known, inspired Cecil Beaton's
costume designs for the famous racing
scene in the film *My Fair Lady* (1964).

LE CRÊPE COMME ARTICLE DE MODE & DE BEAUTÉ

EN raison de la vogue dont jouit cet article essentiel-lement anglais, nous prions tous ceux pour qui la beauté du noir et la perfection du fini sont les premières qualités recherchées, d'exiger le véritable "MYOSOTIS" fabriqué par COURTAULD, et de refuser toute imitation.

Cet article se fait à présent dans un grand assortiment de qualités et de différents prix.

(Marque MYOSOTIS déposée)

SES
APPRÊTS
INTACHABLES
A L'EAU.

FOURNIS PAR TOUTES LES PRINCIPALES MAISONS DE GROS

POUR TOUS RENSEIGNEMENTS, VEUILLEZ VOUS ADRESSER :

SAMUEL **COURTAULD** & Company Limited,
PARIS — 4 -:- Rue de la Bourse -:- 4 — PARIS
R. C. Seine 163.105

**1925 Advertisement
for Courtauld's mourning crape**
Crinkly, dull black crape (spelt crêpe in French) had been used for deep mourning for decades and was the foundation of the Courtauld family fortune. The cult of mourning had reached extravagant proportions during the previous century – largely thanks to Queen Victoria – but after the First World War and the even more devastating Spanish influenza epidemic of 1918, mourning dress fell out of fashion.

1923 Lady Elizabeth Bowes-Lyon
Lady Elizabeth married the Duke
of York – the future George VI – wearing
a simple dress of ivory chiffon moiré
banded with silver lamé and pearls
created by Mrs Handley-Seymour,
a favoured court dressmaker.
The ermine cape was a gift from the
King, the priceless antique-lace veil
and train were lent by Queen Mary.

**1923 Advertisement
for Lux soapflakes,** *The Queen*
A royal wedding was reflected in all
types of media: this contemporary
advertisement pictures a fashionable
bride on her wedding day. The Duke
and Duchess of York's ceremony was
the first to be filmed and the footage
was available the same evening.

Her Bridal Veil and Trousseau

WITH her own dainty hands a bride can keep her veil and all the beautiful things of her trousseau in an ideal state of cleanliness and preservation if she will use Lux throughout the happy years that are to be.

Lux will not harm a silken thread, and the bridal veil, so wondrously and exquisitely made, can be washed without the slightest injury if Lux is used. Lux coaxes rather than forces the dirt from dainty fabrics.

Packets (two sizes) may be obtained everywhere.

Mᵉᵒⁿ de Vertus Soeurs
12 Rue Auber - Paris

c. 1900 Dressing
Complex layers of clothing necessitated the help of a maid with dressing. Many women entered into a lifetime of domestic service, with its own rigid hierarchical structure, in which being a lady's maid was considered a privileged position.

1907 Advertisement for Vertus Soeurs
The ideal body shape at the beginning of the twentieth century was mature and womanly. The 'Grecian', or S-bend, corset pushed the bosom forwards and the bottom backwards and constricted the waist to make it as small as possible.

L'ART ET LA MODE
8, Rue Halévy, 8

XXII. — Nº 22.

Toilette en mousseline de soie peinte de guirlandes de roses et de fleurs bleues soulignées d'un fil d'argent et incrustée de nœuds de velours ciel et de grandes pointes de dentelle. Léger feuillage alternant avec des petits plis au haut de la jupe. Chemisette de Valenciennes ornée d'un étroit ruban de velours ciel.

BRODERIES ET PASSEMENTERIES DE LA MAISON COIQUIL ET GAY, 17, RUE MONSIGNY

c. 1900 Tea gown by Worth
The tea gown, typically a froth of pastel chiffon and gossamer lace, was a relatively comfortable garment worn at home in the afternoon to receive visitors, before changing into formal evening dress. This example by Worth is of chiffon with tamboured net over a satin gown.

1901 Summer toilette, trimming by Coiquil et Gay, Paris, Illustration by Lucy, *L'Art et la Mode*
The delicacy of the Parisian touch is evident in this silk-and-lace summer toilette painted with blue and pink flowers and ribbons. The chemisette, or underblouse, would have had a wired collar to keep it in shape.

1904 Mlle Bresil in tailormade by Redfern, *Les Modes*
The tailormade was the staple of the female wardrobe and could be worn for the majority of daytime activities. This model by the celebrated British firm of Redfern demonstrates the skill required in fitting to the tightly moulded fashionable silhouette.

LES MODES

N° 44   PARIS — LONDRES — BERLIN — NEW-YORK   Août 1904

Photo Reutlinger.

Mlle BRÉSIL
Costume Tailleur par REDFERN

c. 1910 Hat by James Johnson
Vast picture hats were adorned with
flowers, feathers and often entire
birds of paradise as here, despite
efforts made during the previous
century to limit their use. Throughout
the Victorian and Edwardian periods,
animal products were used extensively
for trimming and jewellery: there
was even a craze for incorporating
living pets such as fireflies, beetles
or tiny terrapins that could be fastened
to the body on a length of chain.

1910 Longchamp, Paris
The races at Longchamp near Paris
were, like those at Ascot, important
events in the social calendar and the
place to parade in the latest styles.
Skirt lengths had begun to shorten
by 1910, the trained effect had
disappeared, and the new hobble
style, which fettered the legs,
can be seen on the left alongside
a more practical tailormade.

SALON D'ESSAYAGE

c. 1912 Germaine Schnitzel
The Austrian concert pianist wears
a white Arctic fox fur stole and muff,
comprising at least four pelts. Furs
from North America, Canada, Russia
and Eastern Europe were consumed
in vast quantities.

1911 Fitting room at a fur salon
This sketch shows various types
of fur being modelled, including
ermine, black fox and possibly sable
(after ermine the most luxurious
and expensive skin of all) at a
Parisian salon.

1911 Consuelo Vanderbilt
The American heiress, separated from
the Duke of Marlborough at the time
of this portrait, claimed not to care much
for opulent clothes though she was
regarded as one of the most elegant
women of her time.

1911 *Rita de Acosta Lydig*
by Giovanni Boldini
Mrs Lydig, described by the painter
John Singer Sargent as 'art in its living
form', spent most of her fortune on
clothes: she patronized the Paris house
of Callot Soeurs who made this wisp
of a gown from pink silk and rare
eighteenth-century gold lace.

**1914–19 Rita Lydig's shoes
by Pietro Yantorny**
The consummate Italian shoemaker,
who only made for a few select clients,
created 300 pairs of shoes for Rita
de Acosta Lydig, many using her
collection of rare antique velvets,
damasks, brocades and lace. Each
pair had shoe trees reputed to be made
from wood used in making violins
and they travelled in custom-made
trunks lined with velvet.

THE IMPROVED AMENITIES OF LONDON LIFE—THE ROOF-GARDEN RESTAURANT AT SELFRIDGE'S.

1906 *Cinq Heures Chez le Couturier Paquin* **by Henri Gervex**
Wealthy women flocked to salons such as this one owned by Jeanne Paquin, the first major couturière and president of the *Chambre Syndicale de la Couture* in Paris from 1917 to 1919. Full-length mirrors and windows shed light on clients wearing a variety of summer toilettes, including a tailormade suit, whose wearer carries one of the newest accessories – a handbag.

c. 1909 Advertisement for Selfridges department store
Shopping became a pleasurable pastime, especially at stores such as Selfridges, on London's Oxford Street, where readymade clothing could be purchased. Opened in 1909 on the American model, the department store democratized the shopping experience by marking prices, thus avoiding any embarrassing haggling, and was innovative in providing amenities such as a restaurant and toilets.

Bohemian

'I put on my ancient and historic trousers, which I had worn before the war at parties, with Modigliani's blue jersey. We thought if they wanted a real picture of "Bohemia" we would give them something really good.'

Nina Hamnett: *Laughing Torso* 1932

1916 *Friedericke Maria Beer*
by Gustav Klimt
Beer, a patron of the Wiener
Werkstätte (the Vienna Workshop
artistic community), wears a pyjama
suit in 'Marina' fabric designed
by Dagobert Peche, underneath a
swansdown-trimmed coat. It is not
certain whether or not Klimt designed
garments for the Werkstätte, but his
highly decorative style was clearly a
major influence.

**c. 1905 'Marion' coat dress,
Liberty & Co., 'Dress and
Decoration' catalogue**
Described as a 'Directoire visiting cloak
robe', this A-line coat dress with high,
buckled waist and hand-embroidered
collar and cuffs, defies the currently
fashionable hourglass silhouette.
The style of hat harks back to the
eighteenth century and the hair
is a bohemian shade of red. From
its opening in 1875 in Regent Street,
Liberty of London was a mecca for
'aesthetic' dressers who wished to
express their artistic leanings. The
dedicated dress department stocked
garments and delicately coloured silks
imported from India and the Far East.

c. 1910 Isadora Duncan
The American dancer and free spirit,
strangled by her scarf when it caught
in the wheels of her car on the Côte
d'Azur, wears a flowing Grecian-style
gown, without corset or shoes. Her
brand of natural movement and
flowing dress influenced fashion
designers such Madeleine Vionnet.

1175.

Miss Duncan.

1912 'Delphos' dress by Fortuny

Spanish artist and theatre designer Mariano Fortuny developed a process of creating permanent pleats in silk that he went on to perfect at his factory in Venice, where fabrics have been produced since 1921. His classical Greek 'Peplos' and 'Delphos' gowns, first designed in 1907, together with Renaissance-inspired printed velvet coats, were iconic bohemian dress and are still collectors' items today.

1922 Marchesa Luisa Casati as 'Light' by Worth

The Marchesa Casati was notorious for her dramatic looks, lifestyle and outlandish behaviour. Frequently dressed by her friend Leon Bakst, for this ball in Paris she was costumed by Worth as 'Light' in a diamond-studded net gown against a halo of golden feathers symbolizing the sun. On another occasion, as Saint Sebastian, her electrically wired costume short-circuited and she was unable to attend the ball, sending a telegram saying: 'Milles regrets'.

1910 Hat by Rudolf Kriser
The aim of the Wiener Werkstätte was to integrate the fine and decorative arts to produce *Gesamtkunstwerk*, or the total work of art: architecture, furnishings, fabrics, clothes, accessories (such as this hat), even Christmas decorations, every aspect of human life would be reformed according to its aesthetic principles.

1911 Wiener Werkstätte dresses,
Mode des Wiener Werkstätten Archivs
In 1911 the Wiener Werkstätte set up a fashion department under the direction of Eduard Wimmer-Wisgrill, with some success. The dresses it produced combined the corset-less reform style with Poiret's new Empire line and an emphasis on decoration rather than varied shape.

1913 Emilie Flöge at Attersee
Emilie Flöge, life-companion of Gustav Klimt, ran the fashionable couture house Schwestern Flöge in Vienna. With interiors designed by the cutting-edge architects associated with the Wiener Werkstätte, it catered to wealthy avant-garde women in artistic circles. Her designs for the salon were less radical than the reform styles she wore while holidaying with Klimt at Attersee, which may have been designed by him.
A loose 'hanging' dress is decorated with a panel of folk-style embroidery. Just visible is the pendant designed by Koloman Moser and given to her by Klimt.

c. 1911 The 'Slade Cropheads'
Dora Carrington, Barbara Bagenal
and Dorothy Brett as students at the
Slade School of Art in London were
daring and experimental in their dress.
These young women were among the
first to crop their hair, as their nickname
suggests, as well as wearing trousers,
coloured stockings and sometimes
even different coloured shoes.

c. 1917 *Nina Hamnett* **by Roger Fry**
Also at the Slade, Hamnett would later
become London's so-called 'Queen
of Bohemia'. She is pictured wearing
a dress by the Omega Workshops,
with another of their fabrics seen in the
background on a cushion cover. She
wore a Cubist jumper by Omega in blue,
orange and black during her sartorial
exploits in Parisian cafe society before
the First World War, which also included
wearing workmen's clothing from
the market.

1922 Smoking suit
A pyjama suit with fur-trimmed trousers,
lamé top and fringed scarf is topped
by a bandeau. Women had smoked
in private since the previous century;
in the 1920s 'fast' young women began
to smoke in public. Trousers were still
considered very daring.

Previous spread
1908 Gowns by Paul Poiret
Illustration by Paul Iribe, Pochoir
print *Les Robes de Paul Poiret*
At the beginning of his career Poiret's
designs revived the Directoire and
Empire styles of the early nineteenth
century, in turn inspired by classical
Greek dress. His softly draped, high-
waisted, column-like sheaths were
layered with overtunics and jackets.
Worn with 'antique' hairstyles, they
introduced a new silhouette.

c. 1910 Dress by Paul Poiret
Evening dress of satin overlaid
with a gold tulle peplum and a tulle
overdress embroidered with
polychrome beads and gold thread.

1910 Principals in costume
for *Schéhérazade*
Serge Diaghilev's Ballets Russes
dazzled audiences in Paris and London
from their debut in 1909. Leon Bakst's
sets and costumes fizzed with blazing
Oriental colours and exotic sensuality.
Poiret denied that he was directly
influenced by the Ballets Russes,
but his clothes became increasingly
Oriental in style.

Vera Fokina
Michael Fokin
"Scheherazade."

**1914 'Salomé' dress
by Paul Poiret Illustration by Simone
Puget,** *Gazette du Bon Ton*
Poiret was an impressario: as well as
masterminding a revolution in fashion,
he also fostered a new generation
of fashion illustrators, exhibiting and
promoting their work. By introducing
them to Lucien Vogel, the editor of
Gazette du Bon Ton, one of the most
iconic fashion journals ever published,
he ensured that images of his clothes
would have maximum impact.

1911 Denise and Paul Poiret
Fashion, fantasy and publicity came
together when the Poirets held their
lavish 'Thousand and Second Night'
party, at which they provided costumes
to any of the 300 guests who had not
arrived suitably attired. Denise Poiret
wears a lampshade tunic over harem
pants, with a turban and aigrette.

"SALOMÉ"

Robe du soir de Paul Poiret

LES CORSETS BON TON.

FABRIQUÉS PAR LA MAISON DE CORSETS ROYAL WORCESTER CIE.

Une Révélation
de Finesse.

**1914 Advertisement
for Bon Ton corsets**
The new silhouette demanded a new
physical ideal. Poiret, among others,
claimed to have freed the bust, but the
straighter line still required an elongated
corset to control the waist and hips. This
would become the girdle and the bust
bodice, soon to be called the brassière,
evolved into a separate garment.

c. 1920 'Zouave' outfit by Paul Poiret
Poiret's exotic lamé 'Zouave' ensemble
combines a delicate beaded and fringed
top with North African-style baggy
trousers. His lavish exoticism did not sell
well in the 1920s and the house closed
in 1929.

iv—LADIES' SUPPLEMENT TO THE ILLUSTRATED LONDON NEWS. —v

Purple and Blue Wigs to Complete the Colour=Schemes of Dresses: Gowns that Express Poetic Ideas

FROM UNTOUCHED INSTANTANEOUS PHOTOGRAPHS SPECIALLY TAKEN FOR "THE ILLUSTRATED LONDON NEWS" BY THE POLYCHROMIDE PROCESS, AT THE DOVER STREET STUDIOS; BY PERMISSION OF MADAME LUCILE.

1. THE PURPLE WIG.   2. THE "À COEUR PERDU" GOWN, WORN WITH A BLUE WIG.   4. A BRIGHT EMERALD-GREEN VELVET GOWN CALLED "SUCCESS,"   5. THE "TEMPLE BELLS" DRESS, IN MAUVE-PINK AND WORN WITH

3. THE "BECAUSE OF YOU" DRESS, WITH WHICH A PURPLE WIG IS WORN.   TO BE WORN WITH   PURPLE WIG.

7. A POEM IN BLUE AND PURPLE : A DRESS WORN

...s during the lifetime of the ill-fated Marie Antoinette the head-dress, with its various motifs, such as the "Sentiment Head-dress," "The Pouf à l'Inoculation " (to celebrate the vaccination ... Louis XVI., so amusingly described in the Life of "Rose Bertin : The Creator of Fashion at the Court of Marie Antoinette "), formed such a central part of the dress of that period, so it ...as now fallen to the famous house of Madame Lucile to revive the idea that the hair should accord with the colour-schemes of modern dress. To this end purple, blue, and even green wigs have ...een chosen to harmonise with the tints of the gowns. Though it is scarcely credible that many will adopt this idea, it cannot be denied that the somewhat bizarre colorations of the hair ...nd themselves well to the artistic tones of the dress. Each dress has its name, and has been carried out to convey a special meaning, as may be seen in the examples which we give on this page, ...ch as—No. 2, the "A Coeur Perdu," a draped gown in scarlet chiffon with an Egyptian belt of Wedgwood-blue stones, cameos, and dull silver.—No. 3, the "Because of You " evening

...dress, is carried out in black over purple, with a design of old-gold thread down the centre front. It has an Oriental waist-b... ...forming a loose-knotted end, and finished with a spray of silk hand-made flowers in Oriental shades. No. 4, the "Success" g... ...forms graceful draperies, and is faced back with a soft tone of blue velvet. No. 5, "The Temple Bells," is a dress in mau... ...a bind of orange. The satin bodice is draped with silver lace - embroidered bells, the chiffon sleeves are bordered with tiny... ...browny-pink and silver brocade.—No. 7 is a gracefully draped chiffon velvet gown in a soft shade of blue with gold-and-black... ...waistband is made of a dull brown pink brocade with a touch of bright emerald-green, and the ornament placed at the side...

1913 'Gowns that Express Poetic Ideas' by Lucile

A selection of gowns by Lucile (English designer Lady Duff Gordon) with coordinating coloured wigs. Each gown is named: 'Because of You', 'Success', 'The Temple Bells', 'A Poem in Blue and Purple' and 'A Coeur Perdu (no.2)' – the latter a creation of draped red chiffon with an Eygptian belt of Wedgwood-blue stones, cameos and silver.

c. 1917 Show at Lucile's salon in New York

Lucile claimed to be the first designer to stage live mannequin shows. Her sultry models, with exotic names such as Gamela and Hebe, imbued her 'Gowns of Emotion' with a theatrical eroticism that ensured publicity for her label.

6. THE BLUE WIG.

LE WIG.

d brocade with touches of green and orange,
one in emerald-green chiffon velvet : the skirt
sfully draped to one side and slit up to show
wers, and the belt is in a queer colouring of
sleeves and the skirt faced with green. The
gold-and-green thread.

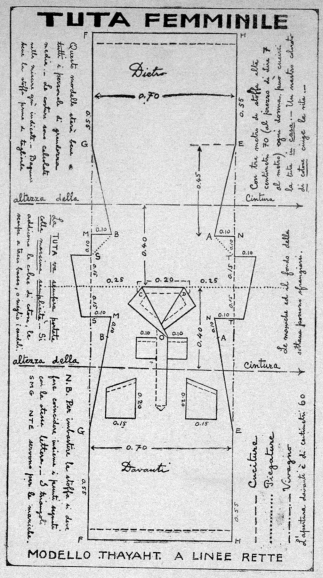

TUTA FEMMINILE

Dietro

0.70

0.55

0.55

Cintura

0.45

0.40

0.10   0.10

0.25   0.20   0.25

0.10   0.10

0.40

0.10   0.10

0.20   0.20

0.15   0.15

0.70

Davanti

Cuciture
Piegature
Voragine

MODELLO THAYAHT. A LINEE RETTE

(Handwritten notes in margins) Questo modello stesso è per tutti i journali di giuntura media. Le colore son chiari nella misura già indicate. Pagina bianca la stoffa prima di tagliarla.

altezza della

La TUTA in questa forma alla massima semplicità. Si addiziona le cifre di oltre, la stampa a taia tessa, o meglio i sandali.

altezza della

N.B. Per imbastire la stoffa si deve far coincidere insieme i punti eguali con la stessa lettera: S S angoli SMG NTE servono per le maniche.

Con tre metri di stoffa alta centim. 70 (al prezzo di Lire 7 al metro) ogni donna può cucirsi la tuta in casa. – Un metro oltre di cotone esige la vita.

Le maschile ed il fondo della cintura possono sfrangiarsi.

L'apertura davanti è di centim. 60

.THAYAHT.

Avvertimenti alle "tutiste„

Negli ultimi vent'anni, il costume maschile è stato di una rigidità quasi inamidata ed i tessuti che hanno servito a coprirci, sono stati preferibilmente di colore scuro ed incerto, per non far vedere la polvere e le macchie.

La maggior parte degli uomini portavano uno stesso abito per degli anni senza farlo lavare.

La «Tuta» è la naturale reazione a questo incredibile stato di cose. La linea morbida e libera, il tessuto lavabile, la semplicità della fattura, la varietà e purezza dei colori, sono altrettanti attributi che fanno del nuovo indumento l'abito razionale moderno, e rompe definitivamente le stupide convenzioni del passato.

Invece il vestito femminile, è stato negli ultimi dieci anni quasi sempre assai semplice e niente affatto rigido. Per la donna, dunque, la «Tuta» non rappresenta che una maggiore semplificazione e l'abolizione totale delle stoffe inutilmente costose.

L'eleganza, infatti, non ha niente a che fare colla qualità della stoffa; e non vi è nulla di più ridicolo, di credere che una stoffa di prezzo possa conferire a chi l'indossa, un'apparenza di grazia o di distinzione.

La donna Tutista deve cercare di abolire tutto quello che è vana esteriorità, cercando nella massima semplicità la vera bellezza.

La «Tuta» femminile può essere orlata di nastro di cotone o bianco o nero alle maniche, alle tasche e al collo. Oppure semplicemente orlata; si porta con un semplice nastro alla vita e senza cappello. Anche una cintura è indicata. Quella donna che avrà poi il coraggio di abolire i tacchi alti, sarà veramente una pioniera nel mondo dell'igiene e dell'arte. Se le ragazze andassero senza tacchi fino a circa l'età di vent'anni guadagnerebbero molto nello sviluppo e nella salute e non avrebbero bisogno di ricorrere ad una finzione antiestetica per accrescere artificialmente la propria statura.

THAYAHT.

1920 'Tuta' by Thayaht, *La Nazione*
Despite the lofty pronouncements
of the Futurists on dress, Thayaht's 'Tuta'
(originally a trousered outfit for men)
was an adaptation of American working
overalls, representing the ultimate
utopian garment. Its 'universality,
simplicity, economy and practicality'
were supposed to replace the 'disorder'
of fashionable dress.

**2009 Giovanna Mezzogiorno
as Ida Dalser, still from** *Vincere*
For a biopic about Mussolini's mistress,
Ida Dalser, the costume designer Sergio
Ballo recreated a dress by Giacomo
Balla, an artist who designed many
Futurist garments. The colour-blocked,
geometric motifs, like the typography
behind, were designed to create
kinetic effect.

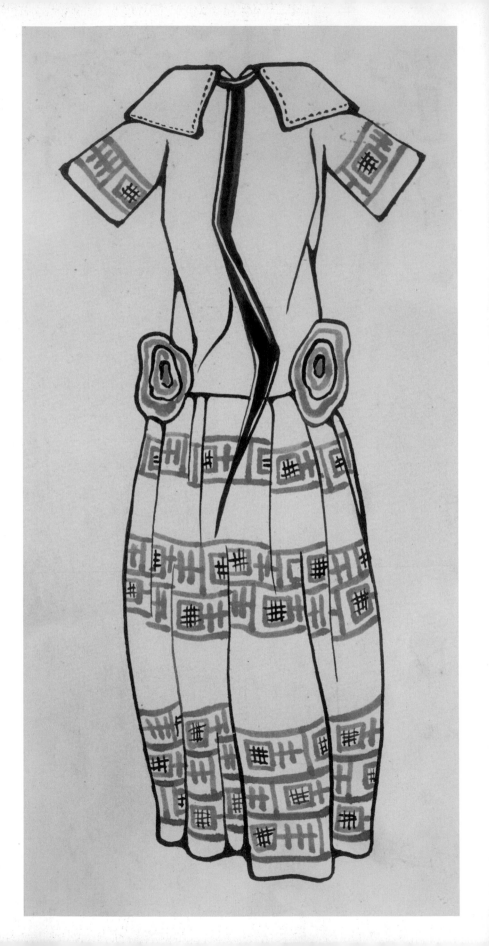

**c. 1924 Dress design
by Liubov Popova**
Attempts by Constructivist designers
such as Vavara Stepanova and Liubov
Popova to revolutionize dress along
socialist principles never took off.
Production was very limited and as
Trotsky himself remarked their more
radical designs did not appeal to the
masses, who continued to crave Western
fashions. This design by Liubov Popova
shows an awareness of the need
to conform to mainstream styles
in order to appeal to Russian women.

**1928 Cover by O. Anisimova,
The Art of Dressing, no. 4**
The garment designs by Anisimova
on the cover of this elitist Russian
magazine blend fashionable and
peasant styles embroidered with
ethnic folk motifs. Nadejda Lamanova,
previously court dressmaker to the
Romanovs, adapted successfully
to the new socialist state, designing
artistic clothes whose Russian-ness
was underlined by the use of
embroidery on rustic materials
such as hopsack and linen.

Uniformity

'The chief items for everyday wear in the businesswoman's outfit are: coat and skirt, blouses, shoes, gloves, hats, a shower-proof or rubber coat, and a long, warm coat for cold weather. With these, she will find herself provided with the essentials.'

Every Woman's Encyclopaedia 1910

c. 1900 Tailormade suit by J. R. Dale
A tweed suit with Norfolk-style jacket made by J. R. Dale, Ladies' Tailor & Habitmaker, who had eleven branches in London. Riding habits, from which the tailormade evolved, had been worn as fashionable dress since the late seventeenth century and were always, as now, made by tailors.

c. 1905 Schoolteacher, USA
The tailormade was the ideal garment
for the 'New Woman' who worked:
it was smart and functional, suitable
for all types of occupations from
teacher to telephone operator.

c. 1900 Woman modelling a hat
The appropriation of masculine style
stopped at the neck: here a stiff-collared
shirt, tie and pin are combined with
a large straw hat trimmed with flowers
and ribbon, worn over a fashionable
pompadour hairstyle.

Overleaf
1900–1910 Factory
workers in Dundee, UK
These factory workers in their timeless
aprons and wooden-soled shoes,
or clogs, could have been photographed
at any point over a period of about fifty
years: only their hairstyles and tightly
corsetted torsos reveal that the image
dates from the early twentieth century.

c. 1900 Seamstress
Isaac Singer's sewing-machine, patented in the mid nineteenth century, had speeded up the process of sewing enormously, but encouraged the addition of ever more trimming and embellishment. The appalling conditions in sweatshops were a matter of public concern and eventually brought about legislation for a minimum wage. Sewing-machines were invaluable in the home: magazines published dressmaking patterns and in America Butterick produced sized patterns from the 1860s.

1927 Hand-knitting in Ardara, Ireland
Village communities all round the British Isles and in Ireland had supplemented family incomes by hand-knitting for centuries. There was a surge in popularity of so-called 'jazz jumpers' during the 1920s as well as for more traditional Fair Isle patterns.

1929 Herring girls in Great Yarmouth, UK
Three Scottish girls knit to earn extra income while waiting for the fishing fleet to come in. During the herring season, thousands of women followed the catch round the coast, wearing rubber or oilcloth aprons and wellington boots to process the fish.

c. 1918 Munitions workers, UK
Some women in munitions factories
adopted trousers, not as an expression
of freedom or feminism, but out of sheer
necessity and practicality. Doing dirty
and dangerous work, they were called
'canaries' because the sulphur used
in the shells turned their skin yellow.

1917 *The Sisters* **by Edmund Dulac**
A member of the Land Army, a nurse
and a munitions worker in their various
types of dress. If a specific uniform was
not required, overalls made of sturdy
washable fabrics, such as cotton drill,
could be worn over everyday dress and
the hair kept out of harm's way under
a cap or scarf.

**c. 1917 Trolley-car conductors,
New York City, USA**
After America declared war on Germany
in 1917 women began to enter the
workforce, replacing men who had been
drafted. These trolley-car conductors'
uniforms of belted coat over breeches,
puttees, boots and cap are a mixture
of military and fashionable styles.

1918 Delivering ice, USA
Men's workwear was often adapted for
heavy manual labour in the war effort,
such as the overalls, shirts and caps
worn here to deliver ice. But the freshly
laundered garments, highly polished
shoes and rather glamorous workers all
suggest a posed image for propaganda
or recruitment purposes.

1916 Daywear by Lelong, Maupas and Manby, *Les Élégances Parisiennes*

During the War, the march of fashion continued: the waistline gradually dropped, hems rose to the ankle, skirts were fuller and the body less constricted than before. The long, belted jacket with capacious pockets, worn over a full skirt, was a fashionable style adapted for uniform.

1918 Armistice Day, UK

Members of the Women's Royal Air Force (WRAF) celebrate Armistice Day in London. The loose, belted jackets and shorter, fuller skirts reflect the evolution of the fashionable silhouette. These women worked at all kinds of trades within the force: as aircraft fitters, mechanics and drivers. Breeches or trousers were also worn.

POUR LES VILLÉGIATURES D'ÉTÉ

Chiffons

PAGE 7

**1918 'Pour les Villégiatures
d'Été',** *Chiffons*
A variety of summer styles demonstrates
the gradual simplification of the
silhouette: the red dress in front heralds
the 1920s' tubular style.

c. 1925 Flappers, USA
High-school students in their flapper
dresses and cloche hats, all with bobbed
hair: the waist has disappeared as
all emphasis has dropped to hip level.
Skirts are flounced, pleated or finish
in a decorative hem. Necklines are
round or 'V' with a scarf or flat collar
allowing a single strand of beads
to be displayed effectively.

1927 Cover of *Delineator*
The uniform cloche hat of the 1920s,
given the Art Deco treatment, along
with the jewellery, by American fashion
illustrator Helen Dryden, who also
worked for *Vogue*. *Delineator*, a general
women's magazine, was published
by the Butterick sewing company
in America from 1873 until 1937.

March 1927   25c

Delineator

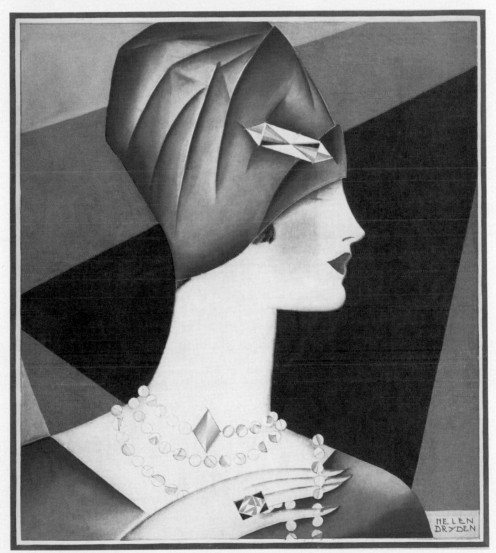

Sophie Kerr
Frances Parkinson Keyes · Eleanor Hallowell Abbott
Smart Spring Fashions

**1920s Advertisement
for stockings, Ladies' Fashions
Mail Order catalogue**
Shorter skirt lengths called for more
appealing hosiery than before. Silk
stockings were available in a variety
of colours to coordinate with an outfit.
Less expensive than silk, so-called
'art' (artificial) silk, renamed rayon
in 1924, was more affordable,
but snagged and laddered easily.

c. 1928 Evening dress
A sleeveless black and silver beaded
evening dress with sunray pattern and
stylized leaves typical of Art Deco style.
Flapper dresses relied for impact
on decoration rather than cut: fringing,
embroidery, beading and feathers
sparkled and shimmered as the wearer
took to the dance floor.

c. 1928 Summer dress
A silk chiffon dress with sections
inserted at the waist to create
an uneven hemline. By the late 1920s,
skirt lengths had dropped well below
the knee. Handkerchief points or longer
set-in sections were much used during
this transitional period.

1937 Duke and Duchess of Windsor
American couturier Mainbocher's
reputation was boosted when
he designed Wallis Simpson's dress
for her marriage to the Duke of Windsor
in France in 1937. Made of blue silk
crêpe, it became one of the most copied
dresses of the twentieth century: not only
was Mrs Simpson notorious for causing
the scandal of Edward VIII's abdication,
she was also a fashion icon.

Overleaf
**1935 Patterns for home dressmaking,
plate from *Modes et Travaux***
Floral prints on long, softly draped
dresses with the waist at natural
level had replaced the 1920s tube
by this May 1935 editorial. Increasing
emphasis on the shoulders with puffed
sleeves, or capes, hint at the wider
shoulders of the 1940s. Skirts are
narrow, bias-cut or pleated and cling
to the legs. Softly waved or shingled hair
under a narrow-brimmed hat completes
the lithe elegance of the silhouette.

Ce crêpe de soie naturelle
vous sera fourni par notre
SERVICE DE NOUVEAUTÉS
au prix de 30 fr. le m. en
1 m. de large. Échantillons
sur demande contre 1 franc.

67

68

69

70

Amazons

'There are two types of fast car: the one that can go from London to the Scottish border in the shortest time, and the one that can carry out a shopping expedition within a five-mile radius of Bond Street in the shortest time.'

Oliver Stewart, British *Vogue* 1930

c. 1938 Kay Petre
Champion racing driver Kay Petre
in the pits at Brooklands racing circuit.
Groomed and glamorous, she was a
celebrity for whom Jaeger designed
a short-sleeved 'dungaree suit' in pastel
silk. Here she wears a boiler suit made
from sturdier fabric; teamed with gloves,
a helmet, goggles, sticking-plaster
and lipstick, she looks stylish even
on the track.

FANCY CYCLING FOR AMATEURS   45

At Emerson's School, Drill Hall, Heath Street, Hampstead.

(a) Backward Stationary Balance

(*a*) and (*b*).   Mount in the usual manner.   When a perfect balance has been obtained, take the match from the

1901 Lady cyclist,
Fancy Cycling for Amateurs
Cycling had been immensely popular since the last quarter of the previous century. It enabled women to take part in group outings and new sports, such as 'fancy cycling' as well as providing an independent means of travel. The tailormade could be worn with a divided skirt; some daring women wore bloomer suits. It seems trick cycling still required a hat adorned with bird-of-paradise plumes, however.

1901 Three women in a Cadillac
Wealthy women enthusiastically took up motoring in the early years of the twentieth century. This required adaptations to existing dress and extra, protective clothing: a long gabardine duster coat, for example, and a veil tied over the hat, both to keep it on and to protect the face from dust, as there were no windscreens in the early days of motoring.

1925 The Debenham sisters
Both sisters wear jazz jumpers, one with a longish skirt and cloche and the other teams hers with corduroy breeches and woolly hat, more practical for motorcycling. Many women learned motoring skills during the war and continued to enjoy them at leisure afterwards.

.THAYAHT. 22

L'ESSAYAGE A PARIS (CROYDON-BOURGET)

COSTUME POUR TOURISME AÉRIEN, DE MADELEINE VIONNET

TRAVERSÉE A BORD D'UN AVION DE "L'INSTONE AIR LINE"

1910 Hélène Dutrieu

Record-breaking Hélène Dutrieu, nicknamed 'The Human Arrow', earned her living as a stunt cyclist, motorcyclist, motor racer and aviation pioneer. Her outfit, a bifurcated skirt or *'aviatrice jupe'*, attached to a tightly buttoned jacket (under which it is said she did not wear a corset) and fitted leather helmet, show that some female pioneers of speed devised specialist garments rather than adapting everyday ones. After the War, masculine-style overalls and trousers were more commonly worn for sports.

1922 Travelling costume by Madeleine Vionnet, Illustration by Thayaht, *Gazette du Bon Ton*

By the early 1920s, passenger flights from Croydon Airport in South London to Paris (via Le Bourget) began to be scheduled. Luxurious surroundings and a flying time of only two-and-a-half hours made for a glamorous day's shopping spree.

1928 Amelia Earhart
Amelia Earhart was the first female
aviator to fly solo across the Atlantic,
in 1932. She disappeared over the
Pacific in 1937. An international celebrity,
she promoted and endorsed a variety
of products including cigarettes and
luggage and produced her own 'Active
Living' clothing line that sold in fifty
stores, including Macy's in New York.
A leather trench coat, breeches, tightly-
laced boots and helmet show a stylish
appropriation of male clothing.

**1934 Swissair stewardess
at Tempelhof Airport, Berlin**
A smart uniform of jacket and divided
skirt with peaked cap worn by the
first female flight stewardess, Nelly
Diener, who was killed in a crash
later the same year.

1900 Skiers, Europe
Since the late nineteenth century, everyday clothing such as these shirt blouses, tailored skirts and hats had been worn for winter sports, as well as an increasing amount of knitted garments. Not until the 1920s did sportswear come to the attention of fashion designers such as Jean Patou, Jane Regny and Elsa Schiaparelli.

1925 Skiwear from La Grande Maison de Blanc, Paris, *Chiffons*
The popularity of jazzy Fair Isle jumpers extended to the ski slopes throughout the 1920s: worn long over coordinating breeches or skirts, socks and gaiters, they demonstrated the versatility of stretchable knitted fabric and its suitability for sports.

Créations de la GRANDE MAISON DE BLANC
6, Boulevard des Capucines

I. Costume en kasha fantaisie et même tissu uni. Bonnet et cravate frange assortie.

II. Costume en kasha à larges rayures et même tissu uni. Bas, bonnet, gants et cravate assortis.

III. Costume en tricot et kasha fantaisie. Bas, culotte, la cravate, bonnet en tissu assorti au ton de la garniture du costume.

I. A fancy kasha costume mixed yellow molleton. Gloves and stockings have both a same kasha revers. A kasha bonnet adorned white buttons.

II. Costume of fancy ziblikasha mixed beige jersey with a kasha scarf with wool fringe. Matching gloves and stockings. Red tricot coiffure.

III. Costume of fancy kasha and red tricot. Coiffure, gloves, scarf and stockings of red tricot.

1912 Riding habit by Redfern
Most women rode side-saddle until the interwar period. The riding habit skirt was cut longer at one side than the other in order to hang evenly when mounted; sometimes warm, woollen jersey breeches were worn underneath. Redfern had been renowned for tailored sportswear since the 1870s.

1938 Erica Popp, *Neue Modenwelt*
German heiress Erica Popp in svelte
breeches and short-sleeved polo-
neck sweater.

1916 Bathing dress
Since the previous century, when sea-bathing had become popular, women had dressed in a costume based on the Victorian sailor-suit to swim. Bloomers and stockings were worn under voluminous tunics. The more streamlined version seen here is made from knitted jersey with a laced front opening, with laced beach shoes and a rubber bathing cap complete with tassels.

**1930 Advertisement
for beachwear from Grand Frédéric
in *Jardin des Modes***
During the 1920s and '30s, tourism boomed, sunbathing became fashionable and a bronzed body a sign of affluence and leisure, not, as before, the sign of a manual labourer. One-piece bathing suits made of elasticated ribbed knits improved fit and exposed as much flesh as possible. Rubber bathing caps and sand shoes were available by the mid 1920s, while espadrilles, traditional French beachwear, were perennially popular.

15 Juin 1930

AU GRAND FRÉDÉRIC

5, Faubᵍ Sᵗ Honoré _ Paris .

365

**c. 1938 Jantzen 'Sunaire'
bathing suit**
By 1930 the American company Jantzen
was the world's leading swimwear
manufacturer, bringing out one
innovation after another, including the
'Sunaire', a top attached to shorts, and
the Shouldaire that allowed straps to
be dropped for an almost allover tan.

1951 Marilyn Monroe
Two-piece swimming costumes were
available from the 1930s, but it was
not until 1946 that the much briefer
bikini was launched, named after
the Bikini Atoll in the Pacific, site of the
American atom-bomb tests of that year.
Marilyn Monroe wears a polka-dot
bikini with frilled overskirt.

Jardin des Modes

Giron

A LA MER
TOUTES LES FEMMES ÉLÉGANTES PORTENT
DES PYJAMAS EN CRETONNE

"LISIÉRES FLEURIES"
FABRICATION PAUL DUMAS
9 RUE Sᵗ FIACRE
PARIS

LISIÉRES FLEURIES

**1930 Advertisement
for pyjamas in Lisières Fleuries
fabric, *Jardin des Modes***
Lounging pyjamas added a note
of glamour to the beach and were
the first trousers for women, apart
from those worn in war, to be generally
considered acceptable. As well as
holiday wear, they were often worn
for relaxing at home.

**1933 Debutantes at the Elizabeth
Arden exercise salon, New York**
The 1930s became a decade obsessed
with physical fitness and body-worship.
The beauty of the ideal physique was
celebrated and women strived to achieve
it through calisthenics and outdoor
exercise, treatments in the beauty
salon and by dieting. In the age
of the machine, the streamlined body
was a requisite sign of modernity.

1906 Tennis match, French Riviera
A short-sleeved blouse (under which the edge of a corset can clearly be seen), full white linen skirt, relatively simple straw hat and flat shoes all would have marked this tennis outfit out as very different from contemporary fashionable dress, but to our eyes, the concessions made to physical exertion are barely visible.

1925 Suzanne Lenglen
French tennis champion Suzanne Lenglen's athleticism was as legendary as her elegance: she was dressed on and off court by Jean Patou, one of the first couturiers to focus on sportswear as a branch of fashion in its own right. He opened a dedicated boutique, Au Coin des Sports, in Paris in 1925.

BEEHIVE KNITTING BOOKLETS No. 10.

PRICE ONE PENNY (or by post 1½d.)

c. 1910 Cover of *Beehive Knitting*
Booklet **no. 10**
Golf was one of the first sports for
which women adapted items from the
male wardrobe such as tailormade
jackets, knitted cardigans and sweaters.
So-called 'sports coats' could be
knitted at home from pattern-books
such as this, or purchased readymade
from department stores. In Britain,
knitting was part of the school
curriculum for both sexes.

1927 Golf fashions modelled
at Moor Park Golf Club, UK
Highly decorative knits on the links:
on the left an embroidered sleeveless
sweater and finely-pleated skirt, and
on the right, a cardigan with appliquéd
crochet geometric motifs. Coordinating
cloche hats complete the practical,
yet stylish oufits.

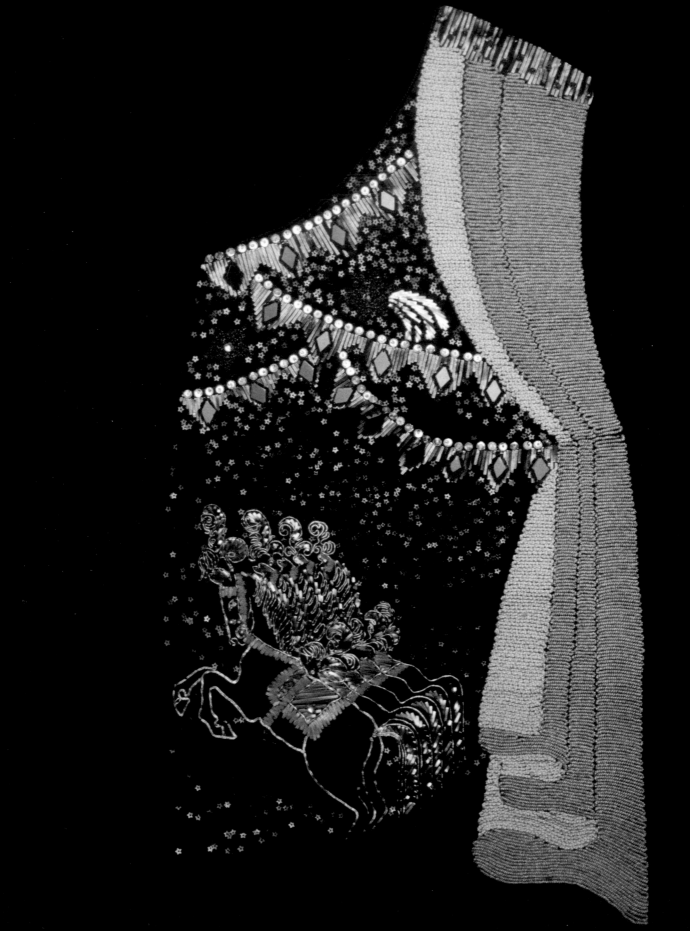

Couturière

'Aha! So now we dress at Schiaparelli,
I see! Whatever next?'
'Cedric! How can you tell?'
'My dear, one can always tell. Things have
a signature, if you use your eyes, and mine
seem to be trained over a greater range
of objects than yours, Schiaparelli – Reboux
– Fabergé – Viollet-le-Duc – I can tell
at a glance, literally a glance.'

Nancy Mitford: *Love in a Cold Climate* 1949

**1938 Embroidery by Lesage
for Schiaparelli**
Schiaparelli experimented with synthetic
materials such as nylon and rayon,
plastics, cellophane and paper. She also
championed the zip fastener, making
it a feature instead of concealing it.
In the late 1930s she launched a series
of themed collections, featuring heavily
encrusted embroidery by Lesage,
such as this example created for her
Circus collection.

ON T'ATTEND !

Robe d'organdi et manteau d'enfant, de Jeanne Lanvin

1920 'On t'attend!', Organdie dress and child's coat by Jeanne Lanvin, Illustration by Pierre Brissaud, *Gazette du Bon Ton*
Jeanne Lanvin began her career as a milliner, but soon branched into children's wear after the pretty but simple dresses she designed for her daughter were admired. By the 1920s she was running a business empire selling couture, perfume, menswear, furs, lingerie, objects for the home and children's clothing; one of the most commercially successful and long-running houses, it is still in existence today.

1925 Evening dress by Jeanne Lanvin
Informed by a passion for art, which she collected, Lanvin's deep-rooted aestheticism set her apart from contemporary modernist designers, as she followed a more romantic and nostalgic approach. Her *robe de style*, a revival of the nineteenth-century crinoline, became her signature garment. This one is embellished with a huge beaded bow motif.

1938 Detail of red wool dinner dress by Jeanne Lanvin
Lanvin was renowned for her exquisite embroidery and beadwork. She collected oriental and antique textiles, using them as inspiration for motifs such as this intricate filigree strapwork of gold leather strips interspersed with silver sequins on the sleeve of a red dinner dress. Lanvin retained two in-house ateliers for her beading and embroidery.

1939 'Cyclone' dress by Jeanne Lanvin
Lanvin's romantic style defied both the 1920s *garçonne* look and 1930s minimalism, but anticipated Dior's New Look, itself based on historical fashion.

1930 Madeleine Vionnet
After apprenticeships with Callot Soeurs and Jacques Doucet, Madeleine Vionnet opened her own couture house in 1912. Best known for cutting on the bias, she created restrained and fluid garments that have achieved almost mythical status, so closely do they symbolize 1930s' modernism. She did not invent the bias cut (Charles Frederick Worth had experimented with it long before) but her methods of draping geometric shapes in endless permutations over a scaled-down, articulated wooden mannequin, were unique.

c. 1931 Sonia in Vionnet
The inspiration Madeleine Vionnet drew from classical Greek dress, seen on ancient artefacts in the Louvre, and her admiration of Isadora Duncan's liberated style, are evident here in fashion photographer George Hoyningen-Huene's image of Vionnet's house model, Sonia, striking a pose in a pair of *crêpe romaine* pyjamas with a whirling scarf behind, like drapery in a painting by Van Dyck.

1938 'The Country, Transformed by Vionnet', Illustration by Edmondson, *Harper's Bazaar*
Even tweeds got the bias-cut treatment from Madeleine Vionnet, as seen in these ultra-smart coat-dresses for country pursuits. The cape on the left, cut on the straight grain, buttons to a matching bias-cut dress; the shoulder cape and skirt on the right are cut on the bias.

1938 Evening dresses by Madeleine Vionnet
Vionnet worked within a muted colour-palette of pastels, flesh tones, silver, gold, black and white that served to highlight her revolutionary technique. Her reputation for guarding her copyright and ensuring good conditions for her workers reflects her integrity, and she is still quoted by many as the 'designers' designer' today.

Les Élégances Parisiennes

COSTUMES DE JERSEY
Modèles de Gabrielle CHANEL (fig. 257, 258 et 259)

1917 Jersey costumes by Chanel,
Les Élégances Parisiennes
Coco Chanel started as a milliner,
but soon opened boutiques in the
fashionable seaside resorts of Deauville
in 1913 and Biarritz, where she opened
her first house of couture in 1915.
These silk-jersey costumes, consisting
of 'jumper blouses' belted over skirts
and blouses, epitomize her easy-
dressing approach.

c. 1927 Dress by Chanel
Chanel's 'little black dress'
hit the headlines in 1926, described
by American *Vogue* as 'The Chanel Ford
– the frock that all the world will wear'.
Now a fashion staple, it was Chanel
who made black chic, transforming
its meaning from grief and mourning,
familiar to so many during the War,
to power and creativity.

1930 Coco Chanel and Duke Laurino of Rome
Always her own best model and publicist, Chanel made her personal style fashionable: she wore trousers, matelot sweaters, bobbed hair, a suntan and costume jewellery mixed up with precious stones. Her energy and drive epitomized the modern woman, but she did not champion feminism, believing that women should dress in order to attract the opposite sex.

1932 Evening dress by Chanel
Chanel's evening wear was as elegantly understated as her separates. A blue chiffon sheath with bias-cut skirt shimmers with irridescent sequins, the only detail a bow motif delineated subtly at the neckline.

**c. 1935 Portrait of Coco Chanel
by Man Ray**
Chanel's spirit and style are captured
perfectly in this photograph. Dressed
in a simple top with a bow at the neck
and a skirt with practical pockets,
a hat tipped over one eye on top of her
immaculately waved hair, she lightens
the almost severe effect by adding
ropes of pearls, snap earrings, bangles
and jewelled cuffs (see opposite).

c. 1935 Cuffs by Fulco, Duke of Verdura, for CHANEL
A pair of silver, gold and enamel cuffs with gem-set Maltese crosses co-designed by Coco Chanel and Fulco, Duke of Verdura.

1955 Marilyn Monroe and CHANEL N°5
Launched in 1921, CHANEL N°5 is possibly the most famous perfume in the world and the first to have a fashion designer's name on the bottle, which she created in modernist style. Marilyn Monroe was famous for wearing the perfume, and numerous celebrities have endorsed it, the current face being French actress Audrey Tautou.

c. 1927 Sweater by Elsa Schiaparelli
Italian-born Elsa Schiaparelli was
self-taught, rather than trained in
fashion, much to the derision of her
contemporary, Chanel. Perhaps this gave
her freedom to be more experimental
and certainly more playful than any
other couturière of her time. Her 1927
collection of sweaters with *trompe
l'oeil* motifs was snapped up by Lord
& Taylor in New York, establishing
an international reputation that was
key to her success.

**c. 1935 Seven outfits
by Elsa Schiaparelli, Illustration
by Pierre Mourgue**
A variety of outfits demonstrates an
aptitude for designing well-cut tailoring,
easy separates and elegant evening
dress not immediately conjured up by the
name Schiaparelli. But there is always
a twist, from the bow ties at the neck,
to the bi-coloured jockey shirt.

**c. 1937 Portrait of Elsa Schiaparelli
by Horst P. Horst**
Framed by Horst to look as if she was
leaning out of an *oeil de boeuf* window,
Schiaparelli wears a tailored jacket
with three-dimensional embroidery
down the front. Her silhouette reveals
the padded shoulders she is credited
with introducing, as well as her surreal,
wavy hat. Her appropriation of art, and
of Surrealism in particular, is perhaps
the best-known aspect of her work.

**1937 'Lobster' dress
by Elsa Schiaparelli**
Schiaparelli's use of Surrealist imagery
reached its zenith in her collaborations
with Salvador Dalí. He created the fabric
for the famous 'Tear' dress, designed
to look like shredded skin, and the
lobster motif on this dress, one of several
outfits purchased by Wallis Simpson
for her trousseau.

1938 Shoes by Elsa Schiaparelli
Schiaparelli's monkey-fur-trimmed shoes
are simultaneously disturbing and erotic
(fur next to skin has been an erotically-
charged artistic trope for centuries)
in the best tradition of the Surrealist
movement. She also designed gloves
with red snakeskin nails, a veil with
beaded blue tendrils of hair and
a hat in the shape of a shoe.

**1938 Advertisement for 'Shocking'
perfume, powder and lipstick
by Elsa Schiaparelli**
Despite her return to Paris after spending
the Second World War in America,
Schiaparelli never regained her position
as a prominent couturière. However,
her iconic perfume, 'Shocking', named
after her signature pink, with its bottle
modelled on Mae West's torso,
remained a bestseller.

Star

'Before Garbo, faces were pink and white. But her very simple and sparing use of cosmetics completely altered the face of the fashionable woman. For a number of years she even used no lipstick or powder at all.'

Cecil Beaton: *The Glass of Fashion* 1954

1929 Louise Brooks
Louise Brooks epitomized the 1920s *garçonne* with her sharp-cut bob. Late in life (she died in 1985) she became a cinematic icon and the inspiration behind Liza Minnelli's role as Sally Bowles in the film *Cabaret* (1972).

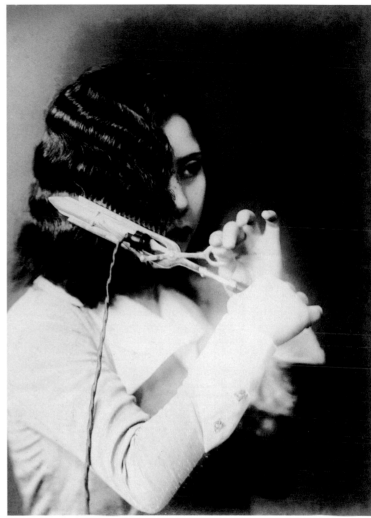

1920s Josephine Baker
The exotic dancer Josephine Baker caused a sensation in 1920s Paris, appearing in nothing but a bunch of bananas and strings of beads for her ironic *Danse sauvage* at the Folies Bergère. Her lavish lifestyle, which included a car painted to match the exact brown of her skin tone, a pet cheetah and glamorous clothes belied a lifelong dedication to civil rights and her work for the French Resistance in the Second World War, for which she was awarded the Croix de Guerre.

1918 Irene Castle
Professional dancers Vernon and Irene Castle stormed over to Europe with the latest American dance crazes, the Turkey Trot, Grizzly Bear and the Tango. Considered one of the best-dressed women in America, the effortlessly chic Irene popularized bobbed hair well before the 1920s and was frequently dressed by Lucile.

**1930s Japanese woman
with Marcel wave**
Trendsetters such as Castle and Brooks, and artistic types bobbed their hair before the First World War. By the 1920s, it was the most fashionable hairstyle worldwide, reaching its shortest length with the severe Eton Crop late in the decade. The 1930s saw a return to longer, softer styles, gently waved with heated Marcel tongs, which had been invented in the late nineteenth century.

1925 Anna May Wong
Chinese-born Anna May Wong
was the first Asian film-star given
major parts in Hollywood. She always
wore 'native costume', as the original
caption calls it, harmonizing with the
craze for Orientalism during the 1920s.
Many couturiers, such as Paul Poiret,
were influenced by Far Eastern styles:
shops such as Babani in Paris imported
Oriental clothing as well as creating
Western-style fashions from Oriental
garments and fabrics.

1937 Girls in *qipao* dresses, China
During the 1920s Shanghai, the
'Paris of the East', became the fashion
capital of China. These young girls
wear Western-style stockings and
shoes, but their hair and dresses are
the height of contemporary Chinese
fashion, which at this time increasingly
reflected nationalism. The *cheong
sam*, or *qipao*, dress has since become
internationally popular.

c. 1925 Evening dress by Premet
A cream silk georgette evening dress
with glass bead embroidery depicting
Chinese-style motifs – these storks,
stylized peony flowers, vases and boxes
show the influence of Orientalism.
The simple, tubular shape, ideal
for heavy beadwork, is given interest
by flying panels at the hem which would
have swung as the wearer danced.

Detail of above

Marilyn Maxwell IN METRO-GOLDWYN-MAYER'S "SUMMER HOLIDAY"

Pan-Cake Make-Up

Which shade of "Pan-Cake" for You

IF YOU ARE A BLONDE
with medium skin, be lovelier with Cream No. 2; if skin lacks color, use Cream-Rose Pan-Cake Make-Up.

IF YOU ARE A BROWNETTE
with medium skin, add glamour with Cream No. 2; if skin lacks color, use Natural-Rose Pan-Cake Make-Up.

IF YOU ARE A BRUNETTE
with olive skin, look your very loveliest with Natural No. 2; if skin lacks color, use Natural-Rose Pan-Cake Make-Up.

IF YOU ARE A REDHEAD
with fair, creamy skin, dramatize your colorings with Cream No. 1; if freckled, use Cream No. 2 Pan-Cake Make-Up.

(For a Sun-tanned effect, Tan No. 1, Tan-Rose or Tan No. 2 Pan-Cake Make-Up.)

for that smooth, young look…

Here's amazing new loveliness for you…right now! Are you a blonde, brunette, brownette or redhead? Select from the Chart the shade especially created for your type. Then try Pan-Cake Make-Up for instant new glamour, for a thrilling, flattering make-up that looks soft and smooth for hours and hours without retouching.

*Pan-Cake (trademark) means Max Factor Hollywood Cake Make-Up

Max Factor ★ Hollywood

Color Harmony Make-Up
PAN-CAKE BRAND MAKE-UP • POWDER • ROUGE • LIPSTICK

1932 Jean Harlow
Madeleine Vionnet introduced the backless evening gown to couture customers in Europe around 1930, but it was not until Jean Harlow appeared in one that it caught on in America. As the original blonde bombshell, Harlow and her platinum waves caused a run on peroxide at drugstores, despite its potentially damaging effects.

1947 Advertisement for Max Factor
Hollywood led the way in developing and popularizing cosmetics. By the 1920s Max Factor, who started as a studio makeup artist in 1908, was selling among other products, his famous Pan-Cake (later known as Pan-Stik) makeup, available in several skin tones. False eyelashes and false nails also originated in Hollywood.

1932 Joan Crawford as Letty Lynton
One of the most commercially successful garments that came out of the movie industry, Letty Lynton's white evening gown designed by Gilbert Adrian, MGM Studios' costume designer from 1928 to 1942, is said to have sold half a million copies in Macy's Cinema Shop alone. The face-framing ruffles are a classic example of so-called 'above the table dressing', designed to highlight the star's face, and the silhouette has also been cited as kick-starting the fashion for wide shoulders.

1934 Maggy Rouff evening gown, cover of *Modes et Travaux*
Many more women would have followed their favourite stars' wardrobes than were aware of the Paris collections. The pattern for the Lynton dress was published by McCall's in 1932: the following year British *Vogue* remarked on the gown's popularity. Its overall style and silhouette, as seen in this evening gown by Maggy Rouff, lingered on for several years.

N.° 352 du 15 Août 1934

Modes et Travaux

Robe du soir
création de MAGGY ROUFF

MARLENE DIETRICH
Paramount Pictures

1933 Marlene Dietrich
Dietrich's blend of European
elegance, ambiguous sexuality and
Hollywood glamour has entered into
the iconography of style. Seemingly
as comfortable in top hat and tails or
furs as in glittering sequinned sheath,
she was credited with introducing
trousers for women to America. Here
she wears a masculine tweed suit with
turtleneck sweater and beret.

1936 Marlene Dietrich in *Desire*
Travis Banton frequently dressed
Marlene Dietrich for her roles.
In *Desire*, she smouldered in silk
and fox furs. Her arched, pencilled-
in eyebrows were widely copied.

55

Late 1920s Greta Garbo
Garbo was uncompromising
and individual in her personal style.
Her athletic figure was ideally suited
to trousers and she rarely wore makeup.
Her natural appearance went against
Hollywood conventions, but nevertheless
she influenced fashion: the millinery
trade was boosted by her appearances
onscreen in various styles of hat.

1935 Sportswear and countrywear,
Modes et Travaux
Checked and flecked tweeds for
sportswear and countrywear, teamed
with flat laceups or brogues and jaunty
hats snapped over one eye, show
the sophisticated, masculine style
that replaced the more youthful and
decorative look of the previous decade.

54. Costume sport en tweed
La blouse est en jersey éco
capuchon. Métrages : 3 m. pe

55. Cette robe est en lai
cruste par une large bague
écharpe en jersey rayé qu

56. Manteau sport en diag
revers en castor et bas de
baguette terminée par un

57. Ce manteau trois-quart
castor, découpé par le mo
heureusement la blouse et

57   58   59   60   61

la jupe se termine par un large pli creux.
la garniture de la cape formant un col
a jupe et I m. 50 de jersey pour la blouse.

jupe-culotte. Au corsage, la découpe s'in-
ui borde le décolleté accompagné d'une
olure. Métrage : 3 m. 25 en I m. 30.

larges poches piquées dessus. Grand col
ustés en forme de hauts parements. Une
dos. Métrage : 3 m. 50 en I m. 30.

ge uni est fermé avec le col rabattu en
nches raglan et les poches. Il complète
57. Métrage : 2 m. 50 en I m. 30.

58. Blouse en jersana fermée par un boutonnage jusqu'au col noué. Les manches
s'incrustent en empiècement devant et dos. Jupe-culotte en lainage quadrillé.
Métrages : I m. 40 en I m. 20 pour la blouse et I m. 80 pour la jupe en I m. 20.

59. Blouse sport en jersana découpée en avant de deux bandes évasées et de pattes
d'épaules se prolongeant sur le haut des manches. La jupe est coupée de deux
sections évasées. Une cape complète cet ensemble sport, vous la voyez représentée avec
les dos. Col revers en astrakan. Mét.: pour la jupe 3 m. et I m. 75 pour la blouse et la cape.

60. Ensemble sport avec cape trois-quarts et blouse tricotée en laine, montée par
un empiècement. La cape est découpée aux épaules par un empiècement fixé par
une patte croisée boutonnée. Jupe droite. Métrage : 3 m. 50 pour la jupe et la cape.

61. Ce manteau droit en velours de laine se boutonne jusqu'au col fait en castor. Une
martingale ajuste le dos. Poches droites assez hautes; les manches larges du haut
sont montées à fronces, elles sont très épaulées. Métrage : 3 m. 25 en I m. 20.

HARPER'

Bazaa
INCORPORATING "VANITY FAIR

OCTOBER–NOVEMBER 1939

FASHION
AS USUAL

Patriot

'Here are some ways in which a man's unwanted garments can be converted to your own use, if you are quite sure he won't want them again after the war.'

The Ministry of Information: *Make Do and Mend* 1943

**1939 'Fashion as Usual',
cover of *Harper's Bazaar***
A model on a rain-soaked Paris street
in a white mackintosh by Schiaparelli
designed to look like a dustcoat.
The strapline sends out an optimistic
message just after the declaration
of war in Europe.

c. 1938 Hitler Youth, Germany
Gingham and flowered prints, lacy
aprons, traditional dirndl pinafore
dresses, long blonde plaits and bronzed,
healthy bodies of girls engaged in folk
dancing represent the ideal of German
womanhood just before the outbreak
of war.

1941 Wartime underwear,
Signal **magazine**
Signal was a lavishly illustrated German
magazine with huge circulation, published
from 1940 to 1945 in many languages,
and a major cog in the Nazi propaganda
machine. This French edition gleefully
highlights the availability of attractive
underwear and stockings in the
Berlin shops.

« Ce joli ensemble revient à 16 marks, explique
la vendeuse; et 6 points seulement. — Rien que 6
points? — Mais c'est magnifique! Je vais l'acheter »

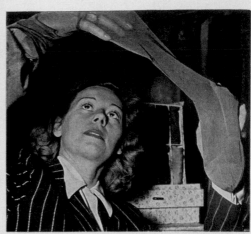

Mais voyons les bas. Un regard critique qui s'y connaît: soie
très fine, très douce; pas le moindre défaut. Les bas viennent rejoin-
dre la combinaison, ce qui décide du sort de quatre nouveaux points

« Regarde combien j'en ai encore! » En riant, la blonde
montre sa carte à son amie. D'un total de 150 points, il lui
en reste assez pour acheter autre chose. Et encore . . .

elle s'est acheté cette robe ravissante avec une jupe si large! Au fond, il ne
lui fallait que des bas, mais quand les femmes se mettent à faire des achats...
la carte de vêtement ne s'y oppose pas. Et les hommes?... Ils y sont habitués

c. 1943 'Service Woollies for Women', cover of *Weldon Knitting Series*

The popularity of knitting and dressmaking at home, by necessity, soared: wool cost less in coupons than as finished garments so knitting was economic, useful and patriotic. Magazines such as *Weldon's* were packed with patterns for warm pullovers, cosy mittens, balaclavas and chilblain-proof socks to wear on duty, all in service colours.

1940 Fitting a corset

Members of the services were provided with a range of practical, if drab, garments: but for many, uniform represented the first comprehensive wardrobe made from good quality materials that they owned. A specially designed corset provided extra pockets for change when the uniform jacket was removed.

Put your best face forward...

To look lovely while you 'look lively' is a big help to good morale,

for good looks and a high heart go together.   Remember, though

Yardley beauty-things usually appear in wartime packings nowadays,

they still have all the qualities you know and trust.

BOND STREET COMPLEXION POWDER
BEAUTY CREAMS · HAND CREAMS
TOILET SOAP (Lavender & Rose Complexion)
LIPSTICK and Refill · ROUGE
TALCUM POWDER (Lavender and April Violets)

They may be difficult to obtain, but they are worth searching for.

If you have any war-time beauty problems write to Mary Foster, the Yardley Beauty Consultant.   She will be very glad to help you.
Y A R D L E Y · 3 3 O L D B O N D S T R E E T · L O N D O N , W . 1

**1940s Advertisement for
Yardley cosmetics**
Looking good was regarded as essential
to the morale of the troops: 'Put your
best face forward...' Manufacturers
brought out lipsticks that coordinated
with uniform, such as Cyclax's 'Auxiliary
Red' for the Wrens (as the UK's
Women's Royal Naval Service was
known). Materials used in makeup,
such as petroleum and alcohol, as well
as paper and plastic for packaging,
were in short supply as they were
commandeered for the war effort.

**1942 USA Women's Army
Auxiliary Corps model uniforms**
Members of the WAAC wearing
uniforms adapted from male styles.
America joined in the War in 1941.
Owing to shortages, insignia and
buttons were made of vegetable ivory
or plastic instead of brass, but despite
this American uniforms were generally
reckoned to be better made than
British ones.

NIC ET LINE   HÉLÈNE VANNER   ALIX

**1939–40 Shelter suit
by Robert Piguet**
Chic shelter suits were designed
by couturiers, although skiwear
did sterling service for most women:
the most important thing was to
be warm. Robert Piguet's wool suit
(possibly an all-in-one siren suit)
with matching hooded cape lined
in checked fabric, fur-lined boots
and compulsory gas mask would
have cut a dash in the air-raid shelter
at the Paris Ritz, fitted out with fur
rugs and Hermès sleeping bags.

**1941 Children's clothes by Nic et Line
and Hélène Vanner, dress by Alix,**
Images de France
Sabots, or clogs, became popular
footwear as people saved leather
or rubber shoes for bad weather or best.
Their history as the choice of disruptive
workers, 'saboteurs', meant wearing
them could also be seen as patriotic in
an occupied country. Alix's summer dress
in (almost) Tricolour stripes sails close to
the wind – in 1942 she was threatened
with closure for using patriotic colours
in her collection and in 1944 her atelier
was shut down for a time after she
flouted fabric restrictions.

marche

LA HAUTE COUTURE PASSE LA LIGNE
REPORTAGE EXCLUSIVITE *marche*

17 MARS 1942
chaque semaine

3ᶠ·
Nº12

LE MAGAZINE FRANÇAIS

1942 'Haute Couture crosses the border', cover of *Marche*
Lucien Lelong organized a fashion show in Lyons in the Free Zone, in which more than twenty Paris couturiers participated, showing solidarity with those in now unoccupied France, as well as attracting buyers from neutral countries. Straight lines and simplicity were the common theme of the collections, although hats were extravagant.

1944 Zazou style, France
A young woman in a coat with padded shoulders, tightly cinched waist, short hem-length and platform shoes. Christian Dior described this style in his autobiography as: 'zazou, half-existentialist, half-zombie' with a 'dreadful mop of hair raised high above the forehead in front and rippling like a mane down the back...'.

**1944 Parisian women wearing
scarf hats**
Hats escaped rationing during the
War: women showed great ingenuity
in creating them out of unlikely materials
such as paper and cellophane. These
turbans made from scarves express the
élan with which French women flaunted
their ability to remain fashionable,
indeed to invent fashion, in the face
of Nazi occupation.

ÉCLIPSE DE RACE

LES SWINGS

1942 *Les Swings*
The swing kids, or Zazous as they
were also known in Paris, ostentatiously
followed American style despite
accusations of unpatriotism and the risk
of physical violence. In the underground
cellar bars and clubs they listened
to the swing jazz of Benny Goodman
and Johnny Hess, considered by the
Nazis to be decadent and subversive.
The female Zazous defiantly wore
excessive makeup and sunglasses,
dyed their hair blonde and ignored
rationing regulations.

1939 Aquascutum three-piece
Original caption: 'Three-piece suit for wartime cycling girl. With the immense increase in the popularity of cycling owing to petrol rationing, dressmakers and tailors are setting out to make suitable clothes for it. Aquascutum of London have produced a three-piece man-made tailored suit in Scutum cloth which is rainproof and windproof. The three-piece consists of a coat, a skirt with three inverted pleats in front, and a pair of trousers zipped at the sides. A girl can thus ride to work, or elsewhere, in trousers and then change into a skirt.'

1940 Hardy Amies and models
Young designer Hardy Amies checking that the length of his skirts conforms to regulations. He was allowed to take time out from officer training to prepare his spring collection for the House of Lachasse. Amies opened his own Savile Row premises in 1946 and became one of Britain's best-known designers.

1942 Utility suit
Members of The Incorporated Society of London Fashion Designers (IncSoc), founded in 1942, were commissioned to design a capsule utility wardrobe. The wool jacket attributed to Victor Stiebel clearly shows the influence of military style on austerity fashion.

1940s Wool suit by Hattie Carnegie
American Hattie Carnegie designed both costly custom-made and good-value ready-to-wear clothing. Known for her trim suits, this example is given interest by the placement of three pockets, the double collar, turnedback cuffs and gilt buttons. Clothes rationing in America generally allowed for more fabric, details of cut and trimming than British regulations. But it is possible that this suit predates rationing in America, as wool was needed for uniforms and the L-85 order, introduced in 1942, restricted the use of natural fibres and banned cuffs.

1943 Land Army girls
The Women's Land Army was vital
in ensuring the continued production
of food. The most distinctive elements
of the uniform were their cotton-
corduroy or wool gabardine breeches.
Also standard issue were khaki cotton-
twill dungarees and overall coat,
a heavy greatcoat, a mackintosh,
cotton shirts, stockings, stout shoes,
gumboots and a hat.

c. 1940 Munitions worker, UK
At the outbreak of the War, women
were once more required to replace
the male workforce. A munitions worker
wears overalls with her hair kept out
of harm's way with a hairnet and scarf.

1943 Delivering bread in Sydney
Dungarees and trousers, or slacks
as they were known, came into
widespread use during the War
for practical reasons. But it would
still be many years before they were
considered fashion garments –
for now, they were simply functional,
a kind of 'domestic battledress'.

**1944 Rationing book,
cover of *Woman's Own***
Clothes' rationing was introduced
in Britain in June 1941 in an effort to
ensure a fair share of available goods.
At first, sixty-six coupons per year were
issued per person, but this number
decreased as the war continued.

**1940 Wartime bride leaving
for church, UK**
Apart from the background of
a bombed-out house, this photograph
shows a radiant bride looking unaffected
by wartime privations. By 1941 silk was
banned for civilian use in Britain as
it was needed to make parachutes.
People sometimes resorted to black-
market deals or replaced silk with rayon,
but many women married in uniform.

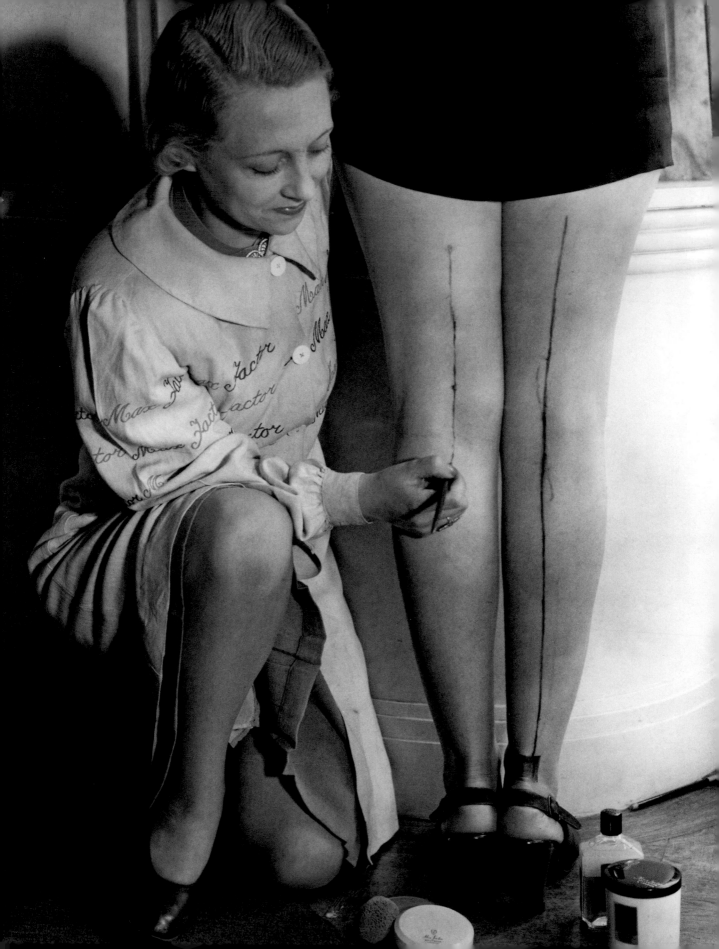

1940 Max Factor stocking paint
Silk stockings became scarce, even
on the black market, and nylons only
became available in Britain with the
arrival of the GIs in 1942. Companies
including Max Factor and Elizabeth
Arden produced leg paint to imitate
seamed stockings, although gravy-
browning and cocoa were cheaper
and just as effective.

1942 Shoes by Salvatore Ferragamo
When economic sanctions were
imposed on Italy in the late 1930s
and he could no longer obtain raw
materials, Salvatore Ferragamo started
experimenting with alternatives, notably
developing the cork wedge sole.
He used plaited cellophane for the
uppers of these examples, and raffia,
tree bark, hemp, paper and fish skin
for other designs.

1945–46 Stage set by Christian Bérard for *Théâtre de la Mode*
When the War ended Paris was eager to reestablish itself as the epicentre of fashion. Over fifty couture houses contributed to a travelling exhibition, the *Théâtre de la Mode*, that attracted thousands of visitors in Europe and America. Wire-frame dolls were dressed in miniature couture garments, complete with accessories and wigs, and placed in tableaux designed by leading stage designers and artists.

1945–46 Jewellery by Cartier for *Théâtre de la Mode*
For the opening of *Théâtre de la Mode* in New York in May 1946, a number of models sported real jewellery in miniature. Cartier's caged peacock plastron, mounted on a Worth dress, was seen to symbolize French couture under the Nazi Occupation.

New Looks

'It is impossible to exaggerate the prettiness of "The New Look". We are saved, becoming clothes are back, gone the stern padded shoulders, *in* are soft rounded shoulders without padding, nipped-in waists, wide, wide skirts about four inches below the knee.'

Susan Mary Alsop: *To Marietta from Paris* 1947

**S/S 1947 'Amour' dinner dress
by Christian Dior**
One of the most commercially successful models of the first New Look collection, 'Amour' was featured on the invitation to Sydney department store David Jones's 1947 French fashion parade, part of its 'Paris Fashions for All' policy, launched in the same year. Australian buyers had been quick to reconnect with Paris couture after the war with annual parades from 1946 and comprehensive coverage of the collections in the press.

S/S 1947 'Bar' by Dior
The signature ensemble of the first
'New Look' collection – Christian Dior's
'Corolle' line – shown in February 1947:
a tailored shantung-silk jacket with
rounded shoulders and padded hips,
moulded to the body over a calf-length
pleated wool skirt measuring eight yards
around the hem and weighing almost
five pounds. Dior's curvaceously feminine
silhouette recalled the nineteenth-
century crinoline and revived complex
traditional couture techniques. For some,
the collection was a breath of fresh
air, for others, it was a profligate waste
of fabric in the face of continued
rationing and austerity.

S/S 1947 'Chérie' by Dior
A navy-blue taffeta, formal afternoon
dress from the first collection. Dior's
garments were so well structured
internally that one wearer declared
it was possible to forgo underclothes.
A stiffened tulle underskirt creates
the ballerina silhouette that Dior
wanted for his 'Corolle' line.

1947 Protestors in Chicago
After the success of his debut, Dior
was invited to America and presented
with a 'Fashion Oscar' by Neiman
Marcus in Dallas. He toured the major
cities where he was greeted with an
equal mix of adulation and protest:
here Chicago women demonstrate
outside his hotel.

**1948 Dior outfit, Illustration
by Jacques Demachy, cover
of *Modes et Travaux***
A short velvet *paletot*, or loose jacket,
embroidered with gold and jewels
from Dior's 'Zig-Zag' collection that
referenced eighteenth-century styles.

Christian DIOR. Fourreau de drap noir complété d'un paletot en velours brodé d'or et cabochons barbares.

ÉDITIONS ÉDOUARD BOUCHERIT
10, RUE DE LA PÉPINIÈRE - PARIS

Novembre 1948. - N° 575. - 30e Année
Prix : **40 francs**
IMPRIMÉ EN FRANCE

A/W 1952 'Palmyre' evening gown by Dior
'Palmyre', a satin evening dress embroidered by Ginesty with pearls, gems and silver thread, epitomizes the use of skilled labour in creating a couture garment. It would have taken several weeks to hand-embroider a dress like this, which was ordered by the Duchess of Windsor, Oona O'Neill (the fourth Mrs Charles Chaplin) and Marlene Dietrich. Post-war, European high society saw a revival of lavish balls, which boosted the couturiers' order books.

1958–60 Roger Vivier shoes for Dior
Roger Vivier perfected the stiletto heel,
the signature shoe of the 1950s and
early '60s. His collaboration with Dior
typified the effort to create a total look,
from accessories to perfume, and
his exquisite shoes, beaded, jewelled
or peacock-feathered, chimed perfectly
with Dior's ethos of craft and luxury.

S/S 1957 'Fuseau' collection by Dior
Dior's mannequins pose in the big salon
at 30 Avenue Montaigne in ensembles
from his last collection. He regarded
them as essential mediators of his vision:
'My mannequins are what gives life
to my dresses, and above all I want
my dresses to be happy.'

**S/S 1958 'Trapeze' line ensemble
by Yves Saint Laurent for Dior**
A grey wool dress and jacket by Yves
Saint Laurent, Dior's young successor,
for his first collection following the
couturier's death from a heart attack
a few months earlier. The 'Trapeze' line
was received with rapturous applause,
but subsequent collections were
considered too daring for the house's
clientele and he left two years later
to serve his time in the army.

1940 Coat by Cristobal Balenciaga
Almost as soon as he arrived from Spain
to set up his Paris couture house in 1937,
Cristobal Balenciaga was acknowledged
as the master of couture, even by Coco
Chanel. Today he is regarded by many
as the greatest designer of the twentieth
century, the so-called 'architect of cloth'.
Shy and reclusive, he ran his house
behind closed doors and despite
charging the highest prices in Paris,
acquired a loyal clientele. Balenciaga's
designs often referenced his Spanish
heritage, as in this brilliant-red wool coat
and Infanta-style feathered headdress.

**1950 Cocktail dress
by Cristobal Balenciaga**
A cocktail dress of shredded silk-
chiffon, veiled coolie hat and evening
coat. Despite Balenciaga's reputation
for severe elegance, he was highly
experimental, carving his coats
and suits out of thick woollen fabrics
with consummate technical skill
and creating dramatic evening-wear
with silks, chiffon and taffeta.

**1951 Evening gowns
by Cristobal Balenciaga**
Balenciaga dedicated his life's work
to the exploration of geometric shapes
on the body. These gowns recall
the sinuous lines of a Toulouse-Lautrec
poster and reveal his gift for dramatic
use of colour, especially black.

**1957 'Sack' dress
by Cristobal Balenciaga**
Balenciaga's 'Sack' line, in which
the garments hang loosely from
the shoulders, away from the body,
was a radical departure from prevalent
hourglass shapes. His austerity suited
the pared-down style of clients such
as the fabulously wealthy Mona,
Countess of Bismarck, considered
to be one of the best-dressed women
in the world. When Balenciaga closed
his house in 1968, she withdrew
to her bedroom for three days.

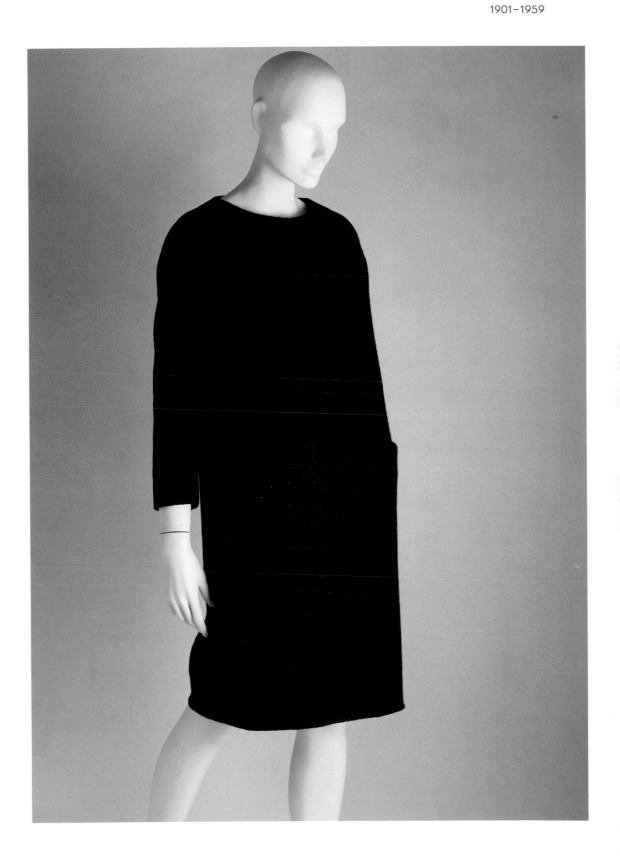

Création de
Jacques FATH

Novembre 1949
31ᵉ Année - Nº 587.

ÉDITIONS ÉDOUARD BOUCHERIT
10, RUE DE LA PÉPINIÈRE - PARIS

Prix : 40 francs
IMPRIMÉ EN FRANCE

**1949 Jacques Fath coat,
Illustration by Pierre Mourgue,
cover of *Modes et Travaux***
Jacques Fath opened his house in Paris
in the 1930s and it remained open
throughout the Occupation. His designs
were known for their bold exuberance,
as seen in this peek-a-boo collared,
loose-fitting coat of soft black wool,
lined and faced with sulphur yellow.

1951 Evening gowns by Jacques Fath
Fath was also known for his striking
evening wear, designed for members
of the elite circles in which he and his
glamorous wife and model, Geneviève,
moved. Complex cutting techniques,
insertions of contrasting fabrics
and elaborate trimming conjure up
a vision of nineteenth-century excess
along the lines of a Winterhalter
painting. Fath's career was cut short
by early death at the age of 42.

**1954 Cocktail dress
and accessories by Pierre Balmain**
A black velvet cocktail dress with
detachable cape of guipure lace
epitomizes Balmain's *'jolie madame'*
style, a style that worked well on screen.
Between 1947 and 1969 he contributed
to many films: stars such as Marlene
Dietrich, Sophia Loren and Brigitte
Bardot became clients.

**1952 Separates
by Hubert de Givenchy**
The aristocratic Hubert de Givenchy's
rise to fame was meteoric – at the age
of 25, in 1952, he garnered acclaim
for his first collection of youthful clothes
in simple fabrics, including this playful
ruffle-sleeved blouse. He trained under
Cristobal Balenciaga, who remained
his mentor and on retirement, directed
Balenciaga clients to Givenchy.

**1956 Audrey Hepburn
in Givenchy in *Funny Face***
Givenchy's career was defined by his
long friendship and association with
Audrey Hepburn, seen here in a publicity
shot for *Funny Face*. Her elfin looks and
gamine figure fitted his youthful style
perfectly, as here in a cropped top,
cigarette pants and ballet pumps (she
always wore flats to minimize her height
– Ferragamo's 'Audrey' pump is still
a best-seller). Givenchy continued
to dress her on and off screen until
her death in 1993.

1953 Elizabeth Taylor in Fontana
Elizabeth Taylor modelling a cocktail
dress in the Fontana Sisters' salon
in Rome, established in 1943. Fontana
dressed many of the stars that came
to shoot movies at the nearby Cinecittà
studios, including Audrey Hepburn,
Anita Ekberg and Ava Gardner; stars
whose clothes on and off screen
introduced the glamour of Italian
style to a wider audience.

1955 Jacket and dress by Carosa,
Harper's Bazaar
Soon after the end of the War, Italian
fashion underwent a renaissance, with
biannual group shows in Florence.
Roberto Capucci, Carosa (Princess
Giovanna Caracciolo), husband-and-
wife team Alberto Fabiani and Simonetta
Visconti, Princess Irene Galitzine (the
originator of 'palazzo pants'), Fontana,
Pucci and Valentino Garavani laid
the foundations of Italian *alta moda*.

1959 Emilio Pucci and models
Florentine nobleman Emilio Pucci
began his career designing skiwear,
and soon became the international
jet set's favourite for his sports
and leisure clothes, such as his classic
silk blouses and Capri pants (his first
boutique was in Capri). Imprinted
with colourful swirling designs, they
predate the psychedelic age.

LONDON'S LINE

Michael Sherard

Digby Morton

FUR-TRIMMED—Michael Sherard edges his grey flecked tweed travelling coat with grey and white rabbit fur—lines it with darker jersey. The suit is in his bright " winter pink," worn with a grey and white striped blouse, red satin tie. Special mention : the handstitched pockets on the suit—capacious one on the coat sleeve.

THE COCOON—This dramatic circular coat has a high scarf collar and curved sleeves, and wraps round to give the cocoon shape. Digby Morton fashions it in velours cloth, in his new bricky colour, Tudor pink. Others were shown buttoning all the way down to a narrowing hem.

LONDON'S LINE
Silhouettes are slim, waisted, with a barrel line

Sigrid

Victor Stiebel

Charles Creed

THE "EXIT SKIRT"—shown above in Victor Stiebel's double breasted tweed dress, brown and white flecked, with fullness in the three back pleats at one side. With tobacco brown goes black. Black leather for the buttons and the shaped belt. Black chiffon for a handkerchief to point the new double pocket. And black velours for the little cloche hat.

THE WAISTCOAT BLOUSE—Charles Creed makes a feature of it. Tucking in like a blouse at the back, but with squared waistcoat fronts, this one is in gold silk shot with pink. Worn under a black velvet suit, trimmed with silk braid. Stiffened and slit hip pockets make the slight "barrel" line. The asymmetric hat is by Vernier.

1950 'London's Line', Morton and Sherard, Illustration by Sigrid, *Woman's Journal*
Digby Morton's tailoring for women, here on the left, was celebrated for lifting the functional to fashionable. Having started as designer at the London couture house Lachasse, established in 1928, in 1930 he set up his own label. Michael Sherard worked under his own name from 1946 to 1965: this neat tailored suit and travelling coat with a pocket on the sleeve and fur trim combine flair and practicality.

1950 'London's Line', Stiebel and Creed, Illustration by Sigrid, *Woman's Journal*
South-African-born Stiebel, whose 'exit skirt' for daywear is seen, reopened his London couture house after the War and became known especially for stylish evening wear. A descendent of the long-established tailoring firm the House of Creed, Charles Creed continued its reputation for quality tailoring.

**1950 'London's Line', Hartnell
and Amies, Illustration
by Sigrid, *Woman's Journal***
Evening gowns by two court dressmakers.
Appointed Royal Dressmaker in 1938,
Norman Hartnell designed much of
Queen Elizabeth II's wardrobe, including
her wedding and coronation gowns,
as well as outfits for the Queen Mother
and Princess Margaret. Hardy Amies
also dressed the Queen and her sister
and was appointed Royal Dressmaker
in 1955. Both were knighted for
their services.

1952 Evening underwear
The hourglass figure with cinched waist
needed body-sculpting undergarments.
Women still wore a girdle or corset,
with a separate bra and a petticoat:
this strapless basque corselette
is designed for evening dress, with
suspenders attached.

LONDON'S LINE

Hardy Amies

Norman Hartnell

BARE BACK. V neck at the back of
Hardy Amies' steel grey satin cocktail
dress "Toledo Blade"—formed by
two draped panels, making one with
the sleeve in front, crossing at the waist
and hanging just below the hem of the
draped skirt—a lovely back line. Embroidered pockets stand out from the
skirt to emphasize the hip. Sleeves are
long, light and wrinkled.

BARE SHOULDER. Half a bolero is better than one—
and supplies the other sleeve on Norman Hartnell's rich
gold satin evening dress "On the Side." Encrusted embroidery on bolero and bodice—rows of copper sequins.
The skirt, drawn across to one hip in an immense bow,
shows the tight, clinging line.

1956 Princess Margaret
Princess Margaret was a beautiful
and fashion-conscious young woman
whose petite figure suited the New Look.
She patronized London designers such
as Hartnell and Amies and also bought
Paris couture, but her wardrobe for
a tour of Africa included this cotton
dress by Horrockses Fashions.

SUNSHINE CLOTHES FOR SUNNY LANDS

1953 Printed cotton dress by Horrockses

The Horrockses' floral cotton frock was a staple of the middle-class Englishwoman's wardrobe from the late 1940s through to the 1950s. With a modified New Look silhouette, well-made and with prints by artists such as Graham Sutherland, they were a must for summer wear; sales were boosted by pictures of the Royal family wearing them, and the rise in package holidays and foreign travel.

1954 'Sunshine clothes for sunny lands', the Queen in Horrockses Fashion, *Picture Post*

Brought up wearing tweeds and simple frocks, the Queen and her sister were adept at mixing couture for grand occasions with less expensive garments from mid-range manufacturers. For her 1954 Commonwealth tour the Queen wore Hartnell and Amies, as well as this summery cotton frock, available from Horrockses' ready-to-wear range at just under £5, although the Queen's version was made to measure.

1954 Miss Virginia Lachasse and her wardrobe

Miss Virginia Lachasse toured the country to raise money for the Greater London Fund for the Blind in the 1950s. She is a miniature wax mannequin now in the Fashion Museum, Bath, whose scale-replica wardrobe from the House of Lachasse gives a valuable insight into the range of garments deemed necessary at the time: from a fur coat to a dressing case of Yardley cosmetics and a packet of coloured cocktail cigarettes.

1955 London debutantes crossing Piccadilly on their way to the Berkeley Ball

The London Season had remained an integral part of society social life after the War and 'coming out' was an important rite of passage that required, for those who could afford it, an extensive wardrobe. However, only three years after this photograph was taken the last debutantes were presented at court, in 1958: against the backdrop of rapid social change, the Season became an anachronism.

1942 'Popover' dress
by Claire McCardell

The 'Popover' was created as an all-purpose housework garment for women who joined the war effort, whether in jobs or looking after the home. Made of denim, with a large, quilted patch pocket on one hip and an attached oven mitt, it could be worn on its own or over other clothes. At only $6.95, it became a runaway success in America.

1946 Shirtwaister dress
by Claire McCardell

McCardell used utilitarian fabrics such as denim, seersucker, cotton, mattress ticking and gingham and became known for her shirtwaisters, such as this example, given interest by the juxtaposition of plain and striped fabric. Her mix-and-match, multi-functional designs were supremely versatile. Trained at Parsons, in Paris and with Hattie Carnegie, Claire McCardell designed for Townley Frocks.

**1947 Evening-wear
by Clare Potter and Dorothy Cox**
Summer evening outfits by two American
ready-to-wear designers: on the left,
a sleek top and pants by Clare Potter
and on the right, a linen dress with
a fitted bodice and soft skirt, both with
pinked edges, by Dorothy Cox. Flat
sandals complete an image of modernity.

1948 Ensemble by Bonnie Cashin
Working in Hollywood as a costume
designer for Twentieth Century Fox from
1943 to 1949, Bonnie Cashin formed
her own company with Philip Sills
in 1953. Her navy-blue and white
polka-dotted 'Eskimo Pants' underneath
a skirt and short jacket, demonstrate
her quirky style.

1948 Tunic dress by Tina Leser
Having started with a holiday-wear
shop in Honolulu, Tina Leser found
success in New York in the early 1940s
with a cotton playsuit that became
a bestseller for Saks Fifth Avenue.
Here a severe jersey tunic dress
is given impact with a metallic belt
and thong sandals.

1949 Evening dress by Traina-Norell
With the growing confidence
in homegrown American fashion, ready-
to-wear designers began to affix their
names to designs. Norman Norell,
who had worked for Hattie Carnegie,
agreed with manufacturer Traina to
take a cut in pay in exchange for his
name being added to the label. During
the 1950s he became known for his
glittering, sequinned mermaid dresses.

1949 Coat by Pauline Trigère
Pauline Trigère was known throughout
her long career for her mastery of
tailoring, particularly in coats. This
dolman-sleeved example, in a bold
check, is cut on the cross with a centre-
back seam to give it plenty of swing.

**1949 Skirt and blouse
by Joset Walker**
A soft, printed blouse with a pleated
bib front is teamed with a long barrel-
shaped skirt, gathered at the waist with
a belt. Embroidered pumps complete
the pretty, fresh sophistication of this
outfit by French-born Joset Walker who
was known for her use of ethnic textiles.
She worked as a costume designer
in Hollywood and on Broadway as well
as for the Theatrical Department
at Saks Fifth Avenue.

**1953 'Four-leaf Clover' evening
dress by Charles James**
Though born in Britain, Charles
James made his name as a couturier
in New York, where he became known
as a virtuoso of complex cut and
construction techniques which created
interest, rather than surface decoration.
The 'Four-leaf Clover' or 'Abstract'
evening dress of cream satin and black
velvet was originally commissioned
by Mrs Randolph Hearst Jr.

**1954 Grace Kelly wearing a dress
by Edith Head in *Rear Window***
With her model figure and ice-cool
beauty, Grace Kelly epitomized all-
American chic. The world was entranced
when she metamorphosed from
Hollywood star to fairytale princess on
her marriage to Prince Rainier of Monaco
in 1956. For her role in Hitchcock's
film *Rear Window* she was dressed by
Edith Head, one of the most successful
Hollywood costume designers, who
won eight Oscars during her career.

1945 *Junior Bazaar*

Junior Bazaar, launched by the Hearst Corporation in 1945, lasted for only three years, but was an influential fashion publication aimed specifically at young girls. With high-quality production values (including early fashion photography by Richard Avedon) and under the direction of Carmel Snow, the magazine indicates the importance attached to a younger market by fashion designers, editors and the media after the Second World War.

1949 *Seventeen* magazine

Seventeen magazine, launched in 1944 and still in worldwide circulation today, was aimed at teenage girls, whose spending power was significant in the post-war period. Along with features on Frank Sinatra, Hollywood gossip and the latest high-school fads, its fashion content reflected the increasing number of American clothes manufacturers developing teenage lines, which were sold in dedicated sections of department stores.

"BARE-SHOULDERED DRESSES" ARE ILLUSTRATED BY TWO BARE-SHOULDERED DRESSES AND ONE WITH SLEEVES

1946 Bobby-Soxers USA

Original caption: 'Bobby-soxers, female half of the more than 6,000 teenagers who today appeared at the 7th Regiment Armory in New York, to enjoy the first of a series of "teen-frolics," surround Benny Goodman whose orchestra gave out with the music for a jitterbug contest. Some of the young ladies hold photos of the "king of swing" waiting for his autograph. Civic groups believe these entertainment programs for young America will help lessen juvenile deliquency.'

1955 Teddy Girls by Ken Russell
Europe took a long time to recover
after the war, as this photograph
by film director Ken Russell shows:
young Teddy Girls pose on a London
bombsite. Jackets, rolled-up jeans
and flats constituted one look, while
the more dressy version of the Teddy
Girl style was an incongruous mix of
neo-Edwardian masculinity, New Look
coolie hats and lace-up espadrilles.

1958 Beatniks, UK
Teenage subcultures were unified
by music – jazz, folk or rock-and-roll –
and by each musical style's shared
sense of dress. Roomy sloppy-joe
sweaters, knee-length plaid skirts,
black stockings, long strings of beads
and dufflecoats (the signature garment
of anti-establishment politics) blend
beatnik and folk styles.

1959 Bazaar boutique, UK
Mary Quant, a product of the post-war
art school system in Britain, opened
her first boutique, Bazaar, in 1955
on the King's Road, which soon became
a meeting place for the 'Chelsea set'.
A new vitality and excitement in art,
design and music, much like that in early
twentieth-century Paris, began to replace
post-war gloom: the old Establishment
ways were challenged by an upsurge
in youth culture, in which fashion
was a catalyst for change.

1960–

1960–

**1965 'Mondrian' dress
by Yves Saint Laurent**
Saint Laurent's 'Mondrian' dress,
inspired by the Dutch painter,
was a huge hit and the ideal canvas
for bold imagery, but its simplicity
led to widespread copying.

By the mid 1950s economic recovery was underway in Europe. Britain's cities may have looked run-down but employment was increasing and with it disposable income and leisure time. Government investment in further education resulted in a dynamic generation of graduates coming out of art and design colleges that challenged the Establishment and contributed to the creation of the image of 'Swinging London'. Regeneration took place across popular culture – in the media, music, theatre and film; furniture and household goods – but it was in the fashion arena that this revolution was most visible: young women no longer wanted to dress like their mothers, but to wear clothes that reflected the youthful, iconoclastic and playful zeitgeist.

Mary Quant was among the vanguard of designers and innovative entrepreneurs in London in the 1950s. Trained in art and illustration, by her own admission she was initially ignorant of the processes of fashion production. But with the daring that comes out of ignorance, she successfully blended the subcultural Mod style with ideas taken from Edwardian school uniform and young girls' dance dress, making simple shifts in informal fabrics, such as poplin, gingham and jersey. Lingerie, hosiery and cosmetics were all given the revolutionary Quant treatment and packaged in black and silver with her iconic daisy logo. Her 1965 tour of America promoted the London Look, as also epitomized by Foale & Tuffin and Barbara Hulanicki of Biba, whose garments were sold in the hip New York boutique Paraphernalia. Fashion shoots in Manhattan with the iconic model of the early 1960s, Jean Shrimpton, and photographer David Bailey; tours by the new breed of British pop groups such as The Beatles and Rolling Stones in 1964; these were all part of the 'British invasion' that took America by storm in the first half of the decade.

In the face of increased labour costs and diminishing numbers of wealthy clients, Parisian couturiers recognised that they too would have to adapt to the emphasis on youth and affordable fashion in order to survive, many introducing prêt-à-porter lines. A young generation, some of whom had trained in the established houses, breathed new life into couture. Yves Saint Laurent showed for the first time under his own name in 1962, a collection that would go down in fashion history. He went on to become one of the most important designers of the second half of the twentieth century, famous for his androgynous trouser suits, revealing semi-nudity and a series of lavish collections in the 1970s inspired by ethnic dress, art, literature and music.

In 1966 he launched his 'Rive Gauche' prêt-à-porter line, sold in eponymous boutiques, that evoked a younger, bohemian *quartier*, as opposed to the more prestigious Right Bank, historically associated with the couture houses. André Courrèges, Emanuel Ungaro, Paco Rabanne and Pierre Cardin were inspired by the Space Age, using synthetic materials. Rabanne created shimmering plastic paillette dresses; Cardin envisaged a future of unisex clothes and Courrèges showed white and silver hipster pants with shoes cut off at the toe and 'eclipse' sunglasses. It is still a matter of debate as to who introduced the mini: Quant's hemlines rose steadily from the start of her career; Courrèges is often credited with its invention in his 1965 collection; but what is certain is that the mini took hold by the mid 1960s and reached its shortest length around 1967. As Christian Dior had said many years before: 'No one person can change fashion – a big fashion change imposes itself.' The difference was that these fashion changes were no longer implemented from on high but came from the street. Most people, including couturiers, recognized by the end of the decade that couture was dead, irrelevant to all but a very few wealthy women worldwide.

New York was having a moment of its own: Pop Art was flourishing, with Andy Warhol's Factory at the core of the action. Paraphernalia, opened in 1965, stocked clothes by British and young American designers who were allowed free reign to be as wild as they wanted. The shop became 'a continuous Happening' where the über-cool gathered against a backdrop of loud music, live dancing models and cutting-edge interior design: by 1966 Paraphernalia had branches all over the States. Throwaway, paper dresses epitomized the pop culture: people didn't want classics any more, but fun, cheap and disposable garments to make an impact at the parties and discotheques of the New York underground scene; some of which even boasted in-house boutiques so that people could change into a new outfit for the evening. More established American designers such as Geoffrey Beene and Rudi Gernreich were inspired by youth culture, the latter stating that he adapted what he saw the 'kids putting together', making it fashion by adding something of his own.

Boutiques proliferated in London. The King's Road provided the in-crowd and pop aristocracy with what Marianne Faithfull, then girlfriend of Mick Jagger, described as 'bright plumage', while Carnaby Street specialized in fast fashion, revolutionizing the retail sector for good. Kensington's Biba became a Mecca for Dolly Birds who spent their weekly wage packet on clothes for Saturday night. Its final incarnation as 'Big Biba', one of the first total-look lifestyle stores, lasted only two years, closing in 1975 due to financial difficulties. The Mod style of the early 1960s had evolved into a softer look, a nostalgic return to Victoriana, Art Nouveau and 1920s decadence, epitomized by Biba's romantic crêpe and satin outfits in sludgy colours, feather boas, floppy hats and vampish makeup.

In 1964 Timothy Leary uttered the immortal: 'Turn on, tune in and drop out', a mantra that became the catchphrase of the hippie counterculture coming out of the West Coast of America. Here, the metallic Pop Art aesthetic was less influential than the psychedelic iconography of the drug, music and communal culture centred in San Francisco, where conspicuous thrift was the order of the day. Antique shawls, vintage uniforms, charity-store finds, American-Indian fringing and outlandish theatrical costume were mixed up and customized with tie-dye, embroidery, crochet, and exotic bells and beads bought on the hippie trail to India – and all imbued with a waft of patchouli oil. Flower Power reached its zenith in 1967, the 'Summer of Love', and the year that The Beatles and Rolling Stones released their homages to LSD: *Sgt. Pepper's Lonely Hearts Club Band* and *At Their Satanic Majesties' Request* respectively. The new generation of couturiers responded by revelling in rainbow colours and swirling textile prints influenced by psychedelic iconography, or by tapping into the traditions of non-Western ethnic dress for inspiration, such as Saint Laurent's 1967 'African' collection. Many designers, as varied as Emilio Pucci, Valentino, Zandra Rhodes, Bill Gibb and others, took on the hippie aesthetic, but the essential DIY nature of the style was difficult to replicate into a designed outfit: the authentic version required the eclectic assembly of garments and accessories

1986 Iman
Somali-born Iman, here in top-to-toe denim, was the first black model to feature on the cover of *Vogue*, in 1979. By the 1980s, designers and brands were engaged in the denim wars, with labels such as Gloria Vanderbilt, Chipie, Stirling Cooper and Fiorucci vying for pole position alongside Calvin Klein, Levi's, Wrangler and Lee.

1986 Hip-hop fans in London
Customized dungarees, baseball caps and sneakers demonstrate the combination of sports and workwear that became the uniform of hip-hop style.

to create something new in a perfect example of bricolage. Despite this, it remains an influential look, constantly revisited in the ever-decreasing cycles of revivals that now characterize much of fashion designers' output. By the end of the 1960s, commercialism had appropriated the hippie culture and many of the 'beautiful people' dropped out: disillusion and cynicism set in with looming oil and economic crises, unemployment, the continuing Vietnam war, student protest, the Black Power movement and struggle for Civil Rights.

In the 1970s, fashion continued to reference the past, from Victoriana to a glamorous interpretation of 1940s style, but also saw a marked increase in the use of denim and sportswear. Previously only worn by working men and children, denim jeans were an item of Americana that filtered into the universal teenage wardrobe during the 1950s through the popularity and influence of Hollywood movies and rock'n'roll stars like Elvis Presley. Soon they were the uniform of youth, endlessly versatile, capable of shifting their sartorial meaning between rebellion, conformity, uniformity, cross-dressing, unisex dressing and eroticism, an everyday staple as well as high fashion, subject even to the hand of the couturier.

Sportswear rose to even greater significance as an influence on fashion in the second half of the twentieth century. The keep-fit craze that began in the 1970s saw garments such as leotards, legwarmers and headbands, previously worn only in the exercise or dance studio, come into mainstream fashion and onto to the disco floor. Donna Karan, who continues in the mould of New York sportswear designers, made capsule collections in comfortable jersey fabrics designed to simplify the lives of working mothers and career women. Her 'body', derived from the leotard, could be worn equally under a shoulder-padded, 'power dressing' corporate suit jacket, or with a pair of comfortable, casual trousers, even jeans. Sportswear made a direct shift into fashion in the 1980s as black hip-hop fans appropriated football and baseball shirts and caps emblazoned with team numbers and logos, a style that brands such as Tommy Hilfiger have exploited and marketed successfully since.

Trainers, shellsuits and tracksuits crossed from the pitch to the pavement to become uniform casual wear. Juicy Couture made the tracksuit a fashion garment, beloved by off-duty celebrities. In the twenty-first century, the greatest advances in textile technology are being made by sportswear manufacturers, from techno fabrics that wick moisture, control body temperature and sculpt muscles, to the Speedo 'Fastskin' swimsuit that imitates a shark's hydrodynamics to enhance performance in the water.

Vivienne Westwood's seminal 'Seditionaries' collection of 1976 blazed the trail for Punk, the first subculture to allow equal rights in dress, behaviour and credibility to women. A sartorial slap in the face, Punk challenged notions of feminine beauty, leading the way to freedom and choice in appearance. Inspired by fetish and bondage wear with some rockabilly thrown in, found materials, body-piercing and fascist symbols, it expressed total antipathy to the hippies' rainbow rags, instead introducing an anarchic iconoclasm and subversion in dress that would never again be as powerful. The more contrived dressing-up of the New Romantics, the dark melodrama of the Goths, the deliberate anonymity of the Ravers, the revisited hippie style of New Age Travellers, even the Kinderwhore slutty look of Grunge would fail to shock following Punk. Westwood's legacy was to make subcultural and street style dress rich sources of inspiration for high fashion designers, from Jean Paul Gaultier to Marc Jacobs, in whose work its influence is evident. During the

2009 Goth Loli in Harajuku
The Lolita and Gothic Lolita, or Goth Loli, styles combine child-like cuteness with Victorian and Rococo-inspired costume. These are among the most popular Japanese street styles and mingle happily with the giant rabbits and superheroes of Cosplay costumes based on characters in manga and *animé* comic strips.

1980s several magazines were launched that tapped into the fertile creativity of London art schools and underground club culture: *i-D* (1980), *Blitz* (1980), *The Face* (1981) and *Arena* (1986) became conduits for a new generation of fashion photographers, editors, stylists and emerging talent such as the young John Galliano, as well as the Japanese designers who redefined fashion in their early 1980s Paris shows. Some of these, including Rei Kawakubo of Comme des Garçons, began their careers in Harajuku, a creative enclave of Tokyo that is home to a vibrant street culture in which a multitude of different styles exists, each with its own complex sartorial vernacular. From the Goth Lolis' child-like Victoriana and the animal characters of Cosplay costumes from manga cartoon strips, to the nineteenth-century school-uniform style of the Harajuku Girls who support Gwen Stefani: stage costume for the street continues to flourish, though not to shock.

By the late 1970s Paris, New York and Milan were the acknowledged fashion capitals of the world. Couture houses diversified and maintained revenue through prêt-à-porter lines and franchises of perfume, sunglasses and cosmetics. Paris itself has survived as a fashion capital because of its historic infrastructure of ateliers and a skilled workforce geared towards the production of couture, as well as the cultural importance with which it regards fashion: it is still seen as the premier stage for the ritual biannual display of fashion, the spring/summer and autumn/winter collections shown during Fashion Weeks.

New York continued the tradition of American sportswear, its sleek minimalism epitomized by Halston and Calvin Klein. Minimalism was also the signature style of Giorgio Armani, who along with Gianni Versace (not known for minimalism), helped to establish Milan as the centre of Italian luxury ready-to-wear. The traditional artisan-based structure of Italy's fashion and accessory companies, often family-run, with close links to technologically advanced manufacturers especially in the yarn and textile industries, gave it a competitive edge over the less agile infrastructure that existed in Britain. London lost much of its dynamism due to the lack of support for designers from the British manufacturing industry: even today much of its talent is destined to go abroad, although it is still regarded as a hot-house of creativity and experimentation. But it is increasingly irrelevant to categorize fashion as country specific: designers resist the notion of a 'Look' applied simply because of their ethnicity; although they may refer to their heritage and culture in their work, indications of nationality are not their aim. From South Korea to Brazil, Italy to Japan, fashion is now a global phenomenon.

Fragmentation and diversity characterize fashion from the 1970s onwards: some designers may be associated with a signature style, such as Halston, Calvin Klein, Giorgio Armani and Jil Sander with minimalism; Gianni Versace, Christian Lacroix and Manish Arora with glamour and colour; Maison Margiela, Viktor & Rolf, Comme des Garçons and Hussein Chalayan with conceptualism, but many, if not all, cross boundaries. Issey Miyake and Junya Watanabe use colour to great effect, while Marc Jacobs is both a minimalist and a colourful historicist.

On the one hand, the fashion world in the 1990s struggled with the demons of postmodernism, which saw its expression in so-called 'Heroin Chic' and a new genre of fashion photography featuring wasted-looking models in seedy hotel rooms; on the other, designers increasingly referenced the past. At Dior, John Galliano evoked the spirit and style of Christian Dior, namely

c. 1965 'Kelly' bag by Hermès
In 1956 a photograph of Princess Grace of Monaco (née Kelly) carrying a Hermès handbag appeared in *Life* magazine. The 'Kelly' bag has since become one of the most iconic and collectable 'It' bags of all time: vintage versions command thousands of pounds.

in his triumphal 1997 debut collection as well as in 2005, when a series of tableaux enacted aspects of the House's oeuvre. Karl Lagerfeld has had more success in updating Chanel's key looks, from chain-linked straps of handbags with double C logo to two-tone shoes, than with collections under his own name or for other labels such as Fendi. Vivienne Westwood forages into the past seeking inspiration, carrying out meticulous research in museums and galleries, resulting in collections that use traditional materials such as tartan and tweed. Britain is also known for designers who add a new twist to traditional classics, such as Paul Smith and Margaret Howell, while Burberry (founded in 1856) has become one of the most-watched British brands of recent years. Ralph Lauren has built a vast retail empire based on the imagined past: his versions of historic Americana from Navajo knits to preppy blazers are displayed in his suitably historicized shops. Dolce & Gabbana have referenced 1960s' Italian cinema as well as icons from 1950s Hollywood: their 1992 'Sack' dress was inspired by a photograph of Marilyn Monroe looking sexy (even) in hessian; the designers directly summoned her presence with an evening dress printed with her blown-up image.

Heritage and tradition are key words in fashion today, assets rather than the drawbacks they were in the 1960s. Many of the world's most prestigious luxury brands (most now owned by vast conglomerates), such as Gucci, Louis Vuitton and Hermès, have long histories going back more than a century and now make clothes as well as accessories and luggage. These brands have maximized the perception and selling-point of their heritage: Louis Vuitton was the driving force behind the 'It' bag obsession of the 2000s; Hermès evokes icons such as Princess Grace of Monaco and Jane Birkin with eponymous handbags designed for them that are still in production today.

Several venerable couture houses have been relaunched or revitalized recently: Worth, Givenchy and Balenciaga among them. Historicism can also be seen in repeated evocations of the style of past icons, from the Marchesa Casati, Audrey Hepburn, Marilyn Monroe and Brigitte Bardot to Jackie Kennedy, whose pared-down look expressed the modern image of the 'New Camelot' and spawned thousands of imitators, her huge 'Jackie O' sunglasses still a fashion staple.

Celebrity has always sold fashion, from royal icons to stars of the stage, screen and musical world: this has not changed since the beginning of the twentieth century, but the global reach of contemporary media ensures fame on an altogether different scale and with it, a wider dissemination of fashion. Once the most photographed woman in the world, Diana, Princess of Wales, ensured success for any designer who dressed her, from the moment of her engagement to the future King to her tragic death. Catherine Middleton's marriage to Prince William will have the same effect. Almost as famous as royalty, Madonna made Jean Paul Gaultier's satin cone-bra notorious during her 'Blond Ambition' tour and personifies Dolce & Gabbana's 'Sicilian Woman' – part saint, part sinner – in their advertising campaigns.

Many fashion designers have become as famous and visible as their clients, no longer hidden behind the doors of the atelier, like Balenciaga, or sitting unseen on the stairs of the salon at shows as Chanel did, but like Tom Ford, surrounded by models in his own advertisements. Fashion models have been replaced on the covers of the glossies and in advertising campaigns for major brands by film-stars and it is now widely acknowledged that the red carpet is more important for publicity than the catwalk, although spectacular

**2009/10 Evening dress
by Dolce & Gabbana**
Referencing a multitude of historical
periods and cultural sources, particularly
Italian cinema and Sicilian style,
Dolce & Gabbana are known for their
celebration of female sexuality and
glamour. Madonna has appeared in
their advertising campaigns as the
'Sicilian woman', a hybrid of saint and
sinner, while here the icon becomes the
dress, in a gown printed with images of
Marilyn Monroe.

fashion shows continue to grab headlines. Actresses, singers and celebrities
fill front-row seats at these shows, rather than the press or buyers, to generate
valuable column inches for the label. Cult TV shows such as *Sex and the City*
and *Mad Men*, which epitomizes the interest in iconic heritage style, not only
advertise real fashion (Manolo Blahnik and Vivienne Westwood, for example)
but also influence fashion. The lines between costume, fashion, celebrity and
influence are blurring: Lady Gaga appears on the red carpet in outlandish
stage costume as well as couture. She was featured on the cover of March
2011 American *Vogue* and her stylist, Nicola Formichetti, has been appointed
creative director of couture house Thierry Mugler, where Gaga is tipped
to collaborate with him on future collections.

The fast fashion world of today, characterized by rabid consumption,
visual overload, a surfeit of choice and an emphasis on self-expression, all
instantaneously mediated through the ether and available to buy with a single
click, would be incomprehensible to an Edwardian woman, but she would
understand fashion's continuing allure. Despite its perceived democratization
and greater accessibility in many respects over the last century, fashion is still
a dictator holding power over our sartorial lives.

Youthquake

'The kids...looked really great, glittering and reflecting in vinyl, suede and feathers, in skirts and boots and bright-coloured mesh tights, and patent leather shoes, and silver and gold hip-riding mini skirts, and the Paco Rabanne thin plastic look with the linked plastic discs in the dresses, and lots of bell-bottoms and poor-boy sweaters, and short, short, dresses that flared out at the shoulders and ended way above the knee.'

Andy Warhol and Pat Hackett: *POPism: the Warhol Sixties* 1980

1966 Twiggy
Sixteen-year-old Twiggy from North London became the face of the second half of the 1960s. Her leggy charm, short bob, painted-on eyelashes and freckles popularized the baby-doll look.

**1960 'Peachy' wool shift dress
by Mary Quant**
Recognizing that young women no longer
wanted to dress like their mothers, Mary
Quant designed witty, modern clothes
with simple lines: pinafore dresses,
skinny-rib sweaters, opaque coloured
tights and a cheaper, mass-produced
line, 'Ginger Group'. Deals with
American manufacturers and outlets
made her one of the most commercially
successful designers of the decade.

**1963 PVC mackintosh
by Mary Quant**
Quant's snappy modern take
on traditional wet-weather gear:
a back-fastening mackintosh,
sou'wester and boots in slick black
PVC, one of the man-made fabrics
that she frequently used.

1964 Mary Quant and Vidal Sassoon
Like Chanel, Quant was her own best
model, embodying her style, with
her Vidal Sassoon five-point bobbed
haircut. In 1965 a promotional tour
of America, during which her models
danced barefoot down the catwalk
to a blast of pop music, was a sensation,
confirming her position as international
queen of the London Look.

1966 Mods, London

Mary Quant took inspiration from the Mods, a group derived from the 1950s Modernists, so-called because of their love of modern jazz. By the 1960s the term Mod was widely used to describe young people of either sex as well as London fashion.

c. 1965 Underwear by Mary Quant

Quant transformed lingerie, hitherto frozen in time, into something sexy and fun: rejecting traditional fussy trimming and pastel shades, she introduced super-stretchy synthetics in strong colours, here a white bodystocking and black roll-on, decorated only with her iconic daisy logo.

quant takes that brilliance to boots!

With quant afoot—boots with a difference in a sparkling first collection of shiny-bright boots by Mary Quant. In crystal clear plastic over colours that zoom into fashion's orbit, they're boots that shrug off wear and weather marks, come up shining. Five different styles, all with the uncluttered, unmistakable Quant touch, all in a choice of colours, all from sizes 3, 3½, right up to 7. The shiny red plastic bag is free—and, for the girl who likes things neat and tidy, there's a quant afoot cotton shoe bag in five different colours for 5/- each. Just watch quant afoot boots start walking, all over town.

1 & 6 'Zip' 6 colours 49/11
2 'Porthole' 4 colours 49/11
3 'Cuff' 3 colours 49/11
4 'Chelseas' 4 colours 49/11
5 'Daddy Long Legs' 4 colours 79/11

quant afoot by mary quant

Mary Quant Footwear Ltd
3 Ives Street, Chelsea
London SW3

TO THE NAKED EYE IT'S A NAKED FACE.

Mary Quant's Starkers.
The make-up that looks like
it isn't there.
You can get it in three
semi-matt skin tones. Bare light.
Bare dark. Bare bronze.
And even if it's hiding
anything, it won't
look as though you have
anything to hide.
To the naked eye.

MARY QUANT

**c. 1967 Advertisement
for Quant Afoot by Mary Quant**
Quant's clear PVC boots with coloured
cotton-jersey linings were playful and
fun, as were the punchy tag-lines for the
groundbreaking advertising campaigns
in which she sometimes featured.

**c. 1968 Advertisement
for Mary Quant makeup**
Waif-like Penelope Tree became one
of the top models of the 1960s. Like
Jean Shrimpton before her, she
dated David Bailey, who along with
Terence Donovan, Terry O'Neill and
Brian Duffy revolutionized fashion
photography. Mary Quant's cosmetics
range, launched in 1966, introduced
the concept of fun and included colourful
eye crayons in a tin, sparkly nail varnish,
light, nude-look foundation and lipsticks
with names like 'Sky Blue Pink' and
'Cool Claret', all in her distinctive
black and silver packaging.

**1965 Jean Shrimpton
at Melbourne races**
Jean Shrimpton, the world's highest-paid model by 1965 and face of the London Look, caused a sensation and kick-started the fashion revolution in Australia when she appeared in a mini-dress without hat, gloves or stockings at Melbourne's Derby Day, the most important event in the social season.

1965 Cathy McGowan
Broadcast every Friday night on British commercial TV from 1963 to 1966, *Ready Steady Go!* was as much a barometer of fashion as for pop music. Its presenter Cathy McGowan, so-called Queen of the Mods, who wore Biba, Foale & Tuffin and her own designs, was one of the new generation of personalities who took the stuffiness out of the media.

**1966 Double 'D' dress
by Foale & Tuffin**
Royal College of Art alumni, Marion Foale and Sally Tuffin opened their boutique near Carnaby Street in 1965. Shift dresses in lace patterned with spots or with playful motifs, and their well-cut suits with hipster trousers, were snapped up by a with-it London clientele and by customers in New York's über-trendy new boutique, Paraphernalia.

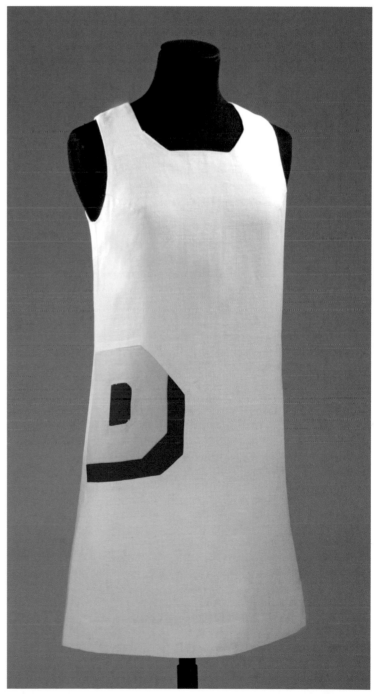

1965 Suit by André Courrèges
Having served a lengthy apprenticeship
under Balenciaga, André Courrèges
launched his own label in 1961.
He stunned the fashion world with
his 1965 collection of super-modern
trouser suits, mini-dresses with skirts
cut four inches above the knee, and
his signature flat white boots with
cut-off toes. He instinctively raised
hemlines in tandem with other
designers such as Cardin and Quant.

**c. 1966 Coats and dresses
by Emanuel Ungaro**
Another protégé of Balenciaga,
Emanuel Ungaro showed his first
collection in 1965. His sculptural clothes
were often made in his favourite stiff,
wool gabardine fabric and in acid-
bright colours. The brand continues
today under American ownership.

1967 Dress by Paco Rabanne
A mini-dress made of mirror Rhodoid discs linked by metal rings. Paco Rabanne's futuristic designs broke new frontiers: determined to create garments without using cloth, he applied his experience as a jewellery designer to materials such as plastic, iridescent rubber, hologram leather, laser discs and optical fibres. In an article for *Marie Claire* in 1967 he declared: 'My clothes are weapons designed for amazons'.

1968 Outfits by Pierre Cardin
During the 1960s Pierre Cardin was also
inspired by space: his 1965 'Cosmos'
collection featured thick tights, skinny-rib
sweaters and futuristic unisex separates
fastened with zips. Bold colour contrasts,
thigh-high boots and over-the-elbow
gloves demonstrate the uncompromising
modernity for which he continues
to be known.

**1967 Trouser suit
by Yves Saint Laurent**
Throughout his career Saint Laurent
was interested in exploring the crossover
of menswear into the female wardrobe.
In 1966 he designed the iconic and
groundbreaking *le smoking*, a formal
trouser suit for women based on
the male dinner suit. His collections
continued to feature trouser suits, such
as this chalkstripe three-piece suit with
tie and snappy hat.

**1969 Safari suit
by Yves Saint Laurent**
In 1968 Saint Laurent introduced
the unisex safari suit: a tunic-style
jacket with open, or laced semi-
open, front, patch pockets and
a belt cinched over trousers.

Previous spread
1965 Opening party at Paraphernalia
Paraphernalia was launched as a stage
for emerging design talent from both
sides of the Atlantic. British and homegrown designers Betsey Johnson,
Deanna Littell, Carol Friedland and Joel
Schumacher were allowed free reign.
At the opening Betsey Johnson,
in trademark silver-foil tank dress,
dances with her own reflection.

c. 1966 Dresses
by Betsey Johnson for Paraphernalia
Geometric motifs on dresses reflect
the influence of Pop Art on fashion.
One of the most inventive of New York's
young designers and still in business
today, Johnson specialized in using
unconventional materials: plastics,
foil, sequin sheeting, creating paper
'Throwaways' and making garments
from paper that sprouted seedlings
when watered.

1966 Edie Sedgwick in Pauline Trigère
Heiress, Factory girl and Warhol's muse,
Edie Sedgwick became a style icon
and darling of the New York psychedelic
scene, here in a Pauline Trigère mini-
dress, ribbed tights and shoes
by Capezio. She became Betsey
Johnson's fitting model.

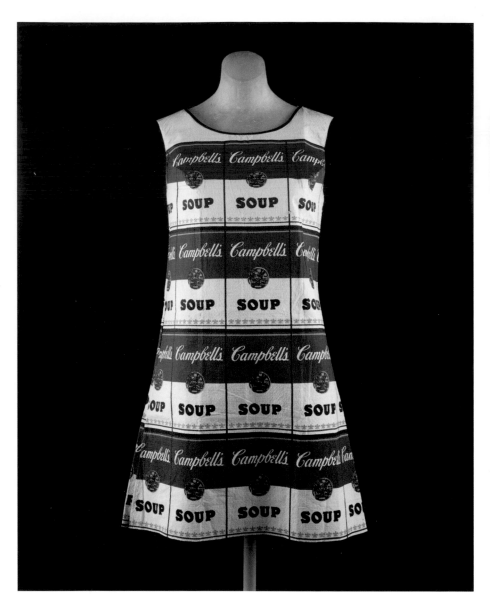

1966–67 Paper 'Souper' dress by an anonymous designer
A paper dress references Andy Warhol's *Campbell's Soup Cans*, exhibited in 1962, one of his 'multiples' comprising thirty-two canvases arranged in a grid, that commented on mass production and consumerism. Advances in textile technology made throwaway paper garments inexpensive and fun.

1966 Boutique at Cheetah Discotheque, New York
The thriving disco culture in New York drove fast-turnaround fashion, as people wanted to wear something different every night. Some discos even had in-house boutiques, such as this one at Cheetah, lined in aluminium, where London design labels including Biba were on sale.

**1967/8 'Football' dress
by Geoffrey Beene**
Launching his own label in 1963,
Geoffrey Beene soon became a success
and is still regarded as one of America's
most gifted designers. This floor-length
sequinned 'Football' jersey dress
displays his playful spirit and love of
American sportswear, but he was also
an innovative cutter, perfecting a dress
with spiral zippers instead of seams.

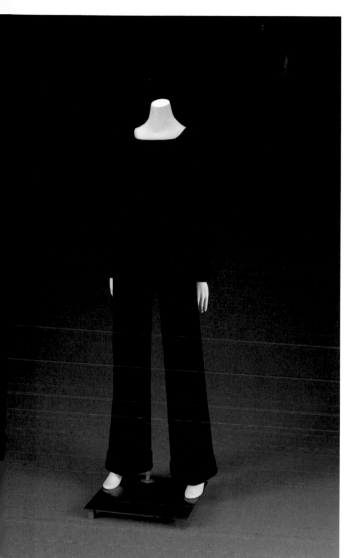

c. 1965 Rudi Gernreich, with models in his designs
An Austrian émigré to California, Rudi Gernreich was a visionary whose aim to liberate women from restrictive clothing was perfectly attuned to the modern American ethos. Innovative designs such as his 1964 topless swimsuit, the unstructured 'no-bra bra' and these topless evening dresses for Harmon Knitwear, gave him both notoriety and publicity. His model and muse Peggy Moffitt is second from left.

c. 1967 Jersey loungewear by Gernreich
Gernreich's headline-grabbing designs overshadowed the appeal of his less controversial easywear: unstructured knitted jersey separates in bold colours and Op Art patterns.

1970 Caftans by Gernreich
These futuristic, unisex caftans worn by male and female bald-headed models were made for the 1970 Expo in Osaka. Gernreich's experimental spirit led him to develop innovations in design years ahead of their time, including spray-on clothes, thongs and Y-fronts for women, well before Calvin Klein.

1966 Carnaby Street boutique, UK
The epicentre of 'Swinging London', Carnaby Street was choc-full of boutiques offering a whole new shopping experience. Music blared out onto the pavements, assistants were young, hip and groovy, and trendy new styles arrived every week to meet the demands of the swarms of Saturday customers. By 1967 it was estimated that there were around two thousand boutiques in Greater London.

1969 Biba catalogue
Biba began in 1963 as a mail-order company: the catalogue, with its moody photography of baby doll models, and bold graphics – especially the iconic logo emblazoned on the cover – was a watershed in this branch of the fashion business. Barbara Hulanicki's designs bridged the Mod look and the growing trend for Victoriana and retro 1920s glamour. The clothes were inexpensive, made from fabrics such as corduroy and satin in a range of muted 'off' colours which she also used for her cosmetics, hosiery and T-shirts.

c. 1974 Twiggy in the Rainbow Room at Biba

After various incarnations including a succession of destination shops that had customers queuing down the street at weekends, 'Big Biba' opened in a former department store on Kensington High Street in 1973, selling the total Biba look: everything from pet-food to children's clothes. An Art Deco gem, it boasted a roof-garden with flamingos and the Rainbow Room, in which Twiggy sits in glamorous sequin sheath with matching mitts.

c. 1966 Coat and dress by Valentino
Amazonian supermodel Veruschka
in a full-length striped wool coat and
chiffon dress by Valentino who, since
the late 1950s until his retirement
in 2007, was at the forefront of Italian
couture. With a glittering international
clientele, Valentino's clothes became
known for their impact, mediated
through his confident use of colour.

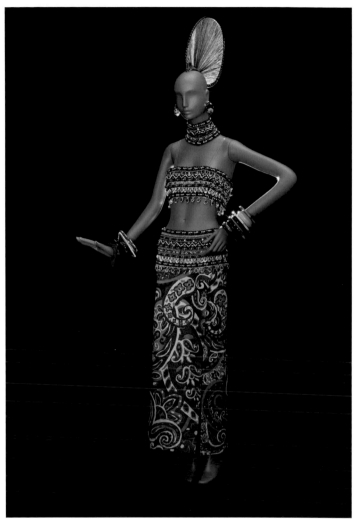

**S/S 1967 Outfits from
the 'African Look' collection
by Yves Saint Laurent**
Throughout his career Saint Laurent
was inspired by ethnic dress: African,
Moroccan, Chinese and Russian
collections were shown during the 1960s
and 1970s. These outfits marry swirling
psychedelic prints with wooden beads
and cowrie shells.

**1967 Jumpsuits, cover
of *Petticoat* magazine**
Teen magazines *Petticoat*, *Honey*
and *19* were launched during this period.
With the increasing popularity of LSD
from 1964, psychedelic iconography
permeated everything from graphic
design to textile prints: the whirling,
amorphous shapes of disco light-
shows translated easily into the visual
language of fashion, as here on these
all-in-one pant suits.

1969 Janis Joplin at Woodstock
Janis Joplin seen here backstage
at Woodstock, the swansong of 1960s'
idealism. Dressed in a kaleidoscope
of colourful tie-dye separates from
the Fur Balloon boutique in New York,
she was the ultimate rock-chick hippie,
mixing satins, velvets and lace with
feather boas and floppy hats.

1969 Dresses by Emilio Pucci
Andy Warhol described it as the
'Pakistani-Indian-international-jet-set-
hippie-look', explored by many designers
during the 1960s and early '70s.
Pucci's diaphanous, colourful caftans
lent themselves to photographic shoots
in glamorous locations, such as here
on the rooftops of Florence.

1969 Clothes by The Fool
The Beatles went into the fashion
business when they opened the Apple
Boutique at their headquarters in
London's Baker Street in 1967. Selling
clothes by Dutch design cooperative
The Fool, whose hippie/gypsy look
is seen here, the boutique closed
after seven months due to poor sales
and an epidemic of shoplifting.

1969 Dress by Ossie Clark
In London the romantic hippie style
was brought into high fashion by a new
wave of art-school-trained designers.
Ossie Clark's sexy, bias-cut, moss crêpe
and chiffon dresses were glamorous and
decadent, as were his beautifully cut
snakeskin jackets. His clothes appealed
to the Chelsea-based glitterati and
pop aristocracy, many of whom hung
out at Quorum, the hip boutique run
by his business partner, Alice Pollock.

**c. 1970 Detail of dress by Ossie
Clark, fabric design by Celia Birtwell**
Celia Birtwell, at the time married
to Ossie Clark, designed his prints –
whimsical 1930s-style floral motifs
that were a major element of his look.
She continues to design, launching
her own clothing ranges for Topshop
in 2007 and John Lewis in 2010.

1970 Dress by Zandra Rhodes
Trained as a textile designer, Zandra Rhodes launched her own label in 1969 and quickly became known for her bold, brilliantly coloured prints, such as this signature squiggle on a chiffon fantasy dress. Inspired by travelling widely, absorbing ethnic influences like these feathered streamers, she is instantly recognizable by her own colourful appearance and bright pink hair.

1970 Twiggy in Bill Gibb
Bill Gibb was the master of mix and match. Inspiration from his native Scotland, medieval and Renaissance motifs and folk/ethnic dress were combined into tapestries of pattern such as this outfit, commissioned by Twiggy to wear at the première of Ken Russell's *The Boyfriend* (1971) in which she starred as a 1920s Flapper.

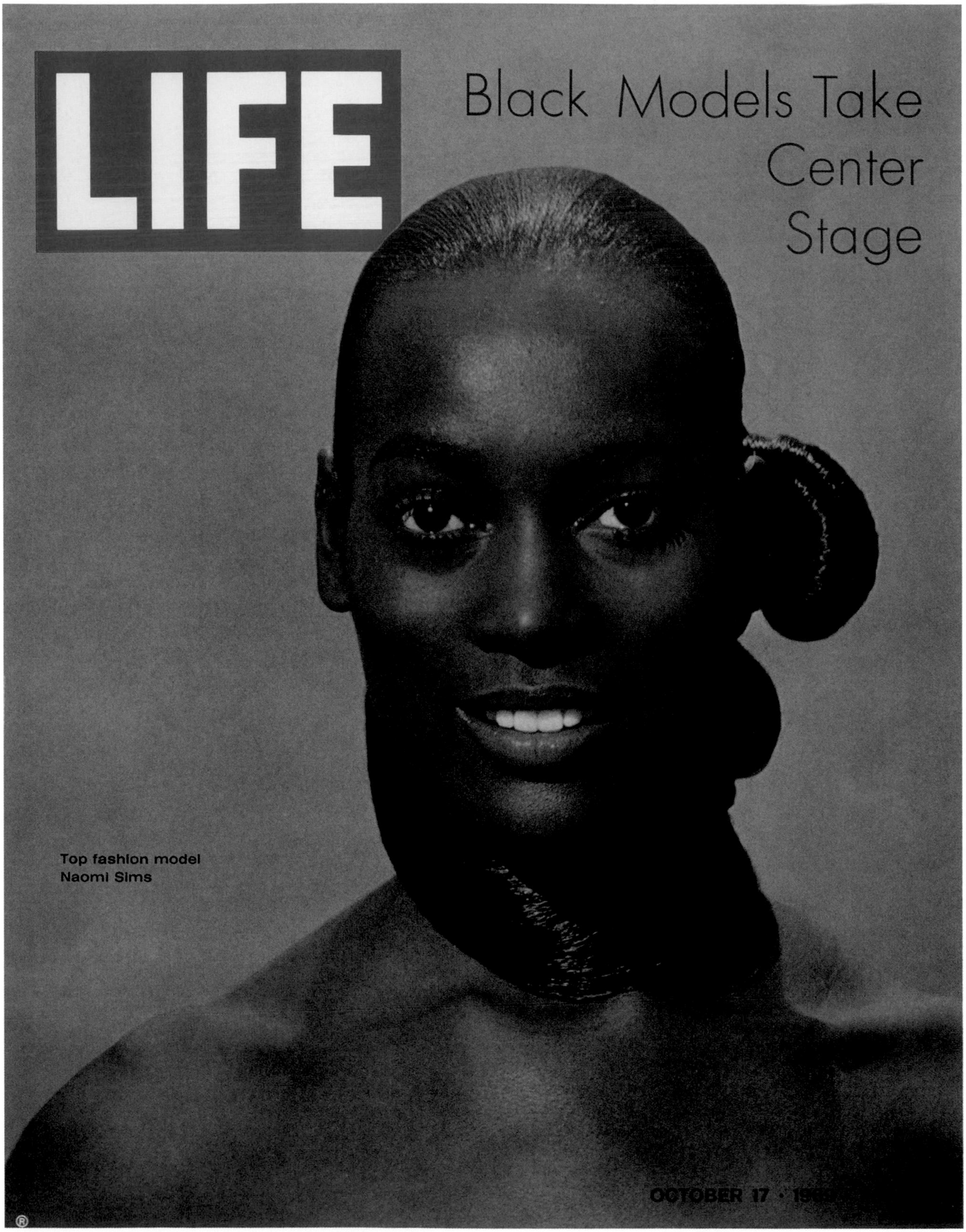

LIFE

Black Models Take Center Stage

Top fashion model
Naomi Sims

OCTOBER 17 · 1969

**1969 Naomi Sims,
cover of *Life* magazine**
The first African-American model to make it onto the cover of a major women's magazine (*Ladies' Home Journal*, 1968), Naomi Sims was an ambassador for the Black is Beautiful movement. She went on to market a line of beauty products for black women. Over forty years later, according to supermodel Naomi Campbell, racial discrimination is still endemic in the fashion world.

1970 Marsha Hunt
Marsha Hunt became a celebrity after appearing in the hit musical *Hair* in 1968, notorious for its nude scene and celebration of 'the age of Aquarius'. Her fringed leather jacket, velvet trousers and chunky ethnic jewellery are in essential hippie mode; her Afro hairstyle reflects the influence of the Black Power movement and her involvement in radical politics while at Berkeley during the 1960s.

1970 Vintage market stall, UK
Self-expression was key to the hippie style: a mix of second-hand (now called vintage), ethnic, customized and shop-bought clothing was more authentic and closer to the ethos of the movement than designer gear that simulated the look. Vintage couture, patchwork, embroidered shawls, beaded Flapper dresses and printed tea-dresses were still easy to find at jumble sales and in markets such as London's Portobello Road.

1970 Outfit by Foale & Tuffin, *Nova*
Foale & Tuffin mixed Liberty prints and
slubby tweeds, quilting them together
in a harmonious blend of colour and
pattern. Nostalgia brought about
a return to crafts such as patchwork,
quilting and hand-knitting, which grew
in popularity throughout the decade.

1973 'The Chic of Araby', *Nova*
Nobody did eclectic and layering
better than Caroline Baker, fashion
editor at the groundbreaking magazine
Nova (published from 1965 to 1975),
who assembled this mix of Moroccan,
Indian, Tibetan and Arabic garments
and jewellery. Her inspired editorials
featuring juxtapositions of designer
and high-street fashion, workwear,
sportswear and street style paved
the way for those in magazines such
as *The Face* in the 1980s.

JEAN SEBERG

Denim and Sport

'You can find bell-bottomed jeans, boot-leg jeans, even flared jeans. But just try to find a regular, trusty old pair of straight-legged denim jeans with no frills.'

Caterine Milinaire and Carol Troy: *Cheap Chic* 1975

1965 Jean Seberg
Although American, Jean Seberg came to define the Parisian Left Bank teenager through her critical success in *nouvelle vague* movies such as Jean-Luc Godard's *A Bout de Souffle* (1959). Her striped matelot top, turned-up jeans and trademark pixie haircut is a look that, like Audrey Hepburn's, is constantly revisited.

1962 Elvis fans, Zurich
Movies including *The Wild One* (1954)
and *Rebel Without a Cause* (1955)
cemented the image of the angst-ridden
teenager and popularized American
casual style. Leather or denim jackets,
jeans, T-shirts, loafers and baseball
boots became the uniform of youth
subcultures. These fans at an Elvis
convention in Switzerland combine
denim with beehive hairstyles.

**1970 California schoolgirls
in unisex style, USA**
California schoolgirls wearing hipster
flares by Landlubber, one of the many
brands that proliferated from the 1970s
onwards. Long hair and jeans, worn
equally by both sexes, blurred the
gender boundaries: unisex had finally
come of age – not through high fashion,
but by the adoption of workwear.

1975 Hotpants, UK
By the mid 1970s a sea of denim was
everywhere; the King's Road, once
bastion of trendy boutiques, was now
a strip of shops selling imported jeans.
Hotpants hit the scene, custom-made
and customized.

1980 Two Tone fans, Coventry
Dressed in unisex jeans, loafers,
polo-shirts and braces, these Two Tone
fans reflect the influence of West Indian
music and style in Britain since the late
1940s. Ska, precursor of Jamaican
reggae, was the music of Two Tone.

1982 Skinhead girl, UK
A skinhead revival girl in denim jacket and Ben Sherman shirt with feathercut hair. Originally an early 1960s subculture, which mutated into many different sub-categories, from the racially mixed Two Tone and reggae fans to those on the Far Right. Whatever the politics, the identikit clothes were more or less interchangeable between genders.

2000 'Bumsters'
by Alexander McQueen

Having left Givenchy after four turbulent years, Alexander McQueen continued to grow his own label, gaining notoriety through a series of spectacular shows based on concepts of empowering women through dress. Typically provocative, his buttock-revealing 'bumster' low-rise trousers had caused a sensation at the unveiling of his 1996 'Dante' collection. Here, bumster jeans with cinch-back buckle are teamed with a giant-knit cotton polo-neck sweater.

2006 Ragga girl
at Notting Hill Carnival

Carnival is an important arena for display and performance worldwide: while less theatrical than the costumes, the clothes worn by onlookers also provide a visual feast and wide cross-section of subcultural street styles, such as this ragga girl's razored denims. More ostentatious than reggae in music and dress, ragga is deliberately provocative, comprising a wardrobe of scanty bra tops, string vests, ripped jeans, revealing shorts or 'batty riders', fishnets and dyed wigs.

**S/S 2007 Dresses
by Jean Paul Gaultier**
Jean Paul Gaultier has always been
inspired by workwear: his signature
matelot sailor top and a strapless
denim bustier here morph unexpectedly
into glamourous evening gowns with
lavish feathered skirts.

**2001 Liberty Ross in advertisement
for 'Twisted to Fit' jeans by Levi's**
The ultimate symbol of comfort,
freedom and gender non-specific
clothing, denim offers endless
opportunities for exploration. Whether
ripped, stonewashed, boyfriend,
engineered, skinny, vintage or designer,
jeans have become a global uniform.

1969 Skiwear by Emilio Pucci
Pucci, an Olympic-standard skier
and keen sportsman, designed
skiwear that combined the glamour
of his famous swirling prints with the
functionality of revolutionary stretch
fabrics, such as Lycra, a synthetic
elastane fibre invented by Du Pont
in 1958.

1979 Jane Fonda
Fonda was the star of the fitness and
aerobics craze that caught on at the
end of the 1970s: her workout videos
sold in millions. Leotards and leggings
in body-clinging stretch fabrics (with
Lycra) began to appear on the disco
dancefloor as well as in the exercise
studio, as the concept of self-fashioning
the body through natural and cosmetic
means took hold.

1981 Norma Kamali
New Yorker Norma Kamali in one of
her own designs from her 1981 'Sweats'
collection. Over-sized shoulder pads
give the utilitarian jersey fabric swagger
and panache. She continues to design
innovative swimwear and multi-use wear
in synthetic stretch fibres: her quilted
nylon 'Sleeping bag coat' has become
a classic.

1985 Body by Donna Karan
Donna Karan's first collection under
her own label, now a major global
brand, was centred around 'Seven Easy
Pieces' designed to simplify the lives
of career women and working mothers.
At a time when corporate dressing
for women imitated masculine clothes,
Karan's looks were feminine and
practical – the key piece was her 'Body',
seen here, a reinvented leotard fastened
with poppers between the legs that
could be worn underneath trousers
or skirts.

S/S 1994 Dress by DKNY
Donna Karan's diffusion line, DKNY,
features easywear separates in jersey
fabrics. A long, zip-front dress reflects
the influence of sportswear and refers
back to Geoffrey Beene's 'Football'
dress from the 1960s.

1987 Salt-N-Pepa
American hip-hop girl group Salt-N-
Pepa mixing baseball jackets customized
with logos, heavy gold chains ('Dukie
ropes') and African textile hats. The
appropriation of sportswear by black
music subcultures grabbed the world's
attention through new media such
as MTV, launched in 1981, and brought
the look to a wider audience, beyond
the housing projects of New York
or Chicago.

1989 NCRU
Hip-hop has been a powerful
influence on fashion since the late
1970s. To the background beat of
the urban ghetto, the B Boys and their
female counterparts, Flygirls, wore
garments previously seen only on
the sports field: oversized sweatpants,
jackets and puffa waistcoats, Adidas
trainers and dayglo-dyed hair are
sported by New York rappers NCRU.

1995 New York schoolgirls in Tommy Hilfiger
Tommy Hilfiger's sportswear-
inspired designs made his label
(and logo) a favourite of hip-hop
and rap stars such as Snoop Dogg.

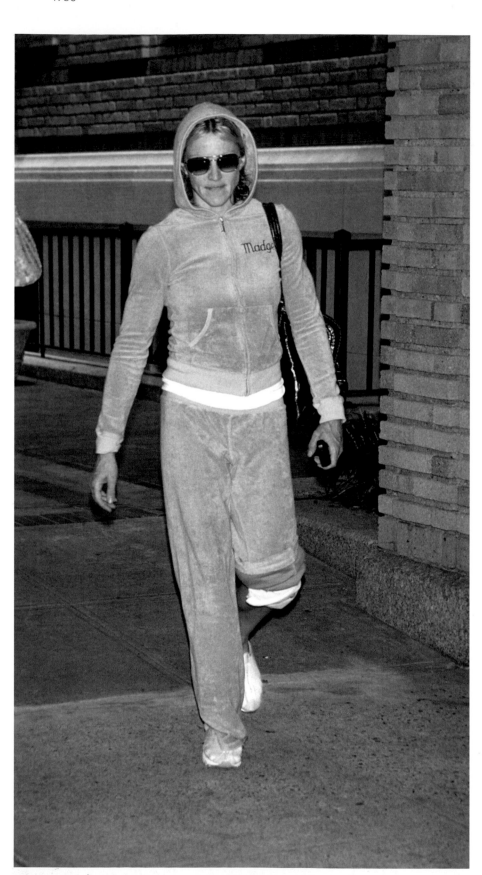

2001 Madonna in Juicy Couture
Tracksuit afficionado Madonna wears her Juicy Couture velour number complete with 'Madge' embroidered in the style of a monogram. The tracksuit, once only to be seen in the sports arena, and having survived its shellsuit incarnation in the 1980s, for a time became almost as popular as jeans for casual wear and, in cashmere, as the ultimate statement of luxury.

1994 Swimwear by Calvin Klein
The phenomenal success of the Calvin Klein brand is based on continuing the ideal of elegant yet sexy modernity in the tradition of American sportswear. 'Calvins' (now synonymous with underwear) for women were launched in 1983: boxer shorts complete with fly opening, they were typically provocative.

2004 'Fastskin' by Speedo
Sportswear manufacturers are at
the cutting edge of textile technology:
Australian swimwear brand Speedo's
'Fastskin' shark suit was developed
using Biomimetics (the imitation of
nature in design) to minimize drag.

**2010 Dress by From Somewhere
with Speedo**
Following a ban by swimming's
governing body FINA (Fédération
Internationale de Natation), the Speedo
LZR Racer, the latest evolution of the
Fastskin suit which had enabled 91 world
records to be broken, was no longer
allowed in competition. Surplus stock
has been upcycled by ethical clothing
designers From Somewhere, whose
limited-edition capsule collection of
'Swimdresses' with strategically placed
logos, provide an environmentally
friendly solution to what would otherwise
have been textile waste.

Outsider

'The only reason I'm in fashion is to destroy the word "conformity". Nothing's interesting to me unless it's got that element.'

Vivienne Westwood: *The Face* 1981

1984 Katharine Hamnett and Margaret Thatcher, *The Face*
In 1984 designer Katharine Hamnett confronted Prime Minister Margaret Thatcher at a reception in Downing Street wearing one of her T-shirts protesting at American nuclear missiles being sited in Europe. She continues to champion many other causes including the eradication of racism in fashion, anti-war and ethical and environmental issues. Slogans on T-shirts remain one of the most versatile forms of sartorial protest and self-expression.

**1976 'Torn Flag' T-shirt
by Vivienne Westwood**
This T-shirt, from the 'Seditionaries'
collection, embodies the anarchic
and confrontational nature of the Punk
movement. Punk, unlike most subcultures
before it, gave women equal status
with men and the freedom to challenge
and confound accepted notions
of femininity.

1977 Vivienne Westwood
Westwood and her shop assistant
Jordan (on left) in bondage gear,
jackets and trousers festooned with
straps. In the early 1970s, Vivienne
Westwood and her then partner,
Malcolm McLaren, ran a series of
shops on the King's Road, selling a
variety of clothing styles, from 1950s
Teddy Boy, to Rocker and sado-
masochistic rubber and fetish wear.
Combining elements from all of these,
the 1976 'Seditionaries' collection,
launched from their shop of the same
name, became the sartorial blueprint
for Punk.

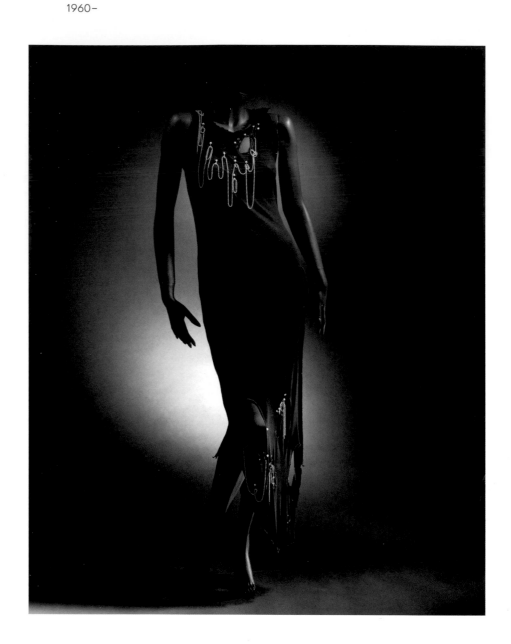

**1977 Dress from 'Conceptual Chic'
collection by Zandra Rhodes**
Like many forms of minority dress, Punk
was soon appropriated by mainstream
and designer fashion. Zandra Rhodes's
dress, with its carefully finished 'ripped'
edges and diamanté safety pins,
presaged the death of Punk, which was
consigned to a tourist attraction on the
King's Road on a Saturday afternoon.

1979 Punks in Piccadilly
Punk was the last authentic
subcultural style. After it, clothing
would never again have the power
to shock: piercings, tattoos, subversive
symbols, weird makeup and dyed hair
now barely command a second glance,
thanks to the trail blazed by Punk.

1980 London Goth
An eclectic mix of bangles, chains
and jewellery, layered and tattered
clothing, dyed hair and deathly shades
of makeup depict the connection and
transition between Punk and Goth style.

1980 Goths at the Batcave, London
Goths gathered at the Batcave, one
of the many clubs on the underground
London scene reflecting the city's
vibrant youth culture, which embraced
music and fashion that was regenerated
by Punk.

2005 Goth in Harajuku
Subcultural fashion has been turned into performance art on the streets of Tokyo's Harajuku. Since the late 1960s this district has been the hotbed of Japanese fashion: many of today's most famous brands such as Yamamoto and Comme des Garçons started there. Teenagers mix Western street style with numerous other influences and customize it into an individual look, such as this befeathered Goth.

1980 Grace Jones
The cross-dressing and androgyny that was an element of Punk, Goth and New Romantic styles came together in the shape of Grace Jones. Queen of the New Wave club scene in the 1980s, her flat-top haircut and Issey Miyake moulded, silicone second-skin bustier bodice express a hard-edged glamour.

FASHION

THE FACE **53**

**c. 1982 Vivienne Westwood
and team**
Dressed in her Spring/Summer
1982 'Savage' collection, Westwood,
McLaren and models pose in their
World's End shop in London. The
layering and decoration of the
collection were typically audacious:
wrapped dresses, skirts over leggings,
'pettidrawers' and shirt-tails appearing
from under shorts; all featured Matisse-
like cut-outs and Native American
geometric motifs. Outsize bowler hats
and tribal face- and body-paint were
worn to match.

**1985 Outfit styled by Amanda
Harlech, *The Face***
The 1980s witnessed the birth
of a new generation of magazines
that challenged the glossies including
The Face, *i-D*, *Blitz* and *Arena*. Mixing
articles on fashion and music with
topical interviews, they employed
many stylists, photographers, journalists
and graphic designers who became
highly successful. An editorial spread
styled by Amanda Harlech, muse
to John Galliano and later Karl
Lagerfeld, scavenges a magpie
collection gathered from market stalls,
young designers and high-fashion
boutiques, epitomizing the eclecticism
of the contemporary look.

1984 Portrait of Letty, UK
Rastafarian dreadlocks announced
affiliation to the New Age of Aquarius:
hippies became better-known as
Travellers, tree-huggers and eco-
warriors who existed on the margins
of conventional society and created
their own eclectic anti-fashion style
of rainbow rags.

1988 Raver, UK
During the second half of the 1980s,
several disparate subcultures came
together in common enjoyment of acid-
house music to dance at illicit raves
and clubs where ecstasy was the drug
of choice. The happy 'smiley' face in
dayglo colours became the logo of the
Ravers, who dressed below the radar
in baggy jeans and T-shirts.

**S/S 1990 'New Age' ensemble
by Rifat Ozbek**
Turkish-born Rifat Ozbek was known
throughout the 1980s for making
ethnically inspired clothes for urban
sophisticates, combining silks, taffeta
and velvets in rich Ottoman colours.
However, in 1990 his all-white 'New
Age' collection referenced the acid-
house club culture: teaming sequinned
bra tops and shorts with anoraks and
bum-bags suitable for an all-night rave.

1992 Techno girl, Italy
As music styles fragmented and
developed from acid-house and rave,
so did the subcultures that went with
them: Cyberpunks and Technos, styles
especially popular in Europe, dressed
in found industrial waste objects,
anti-radiation suits, camouflage and
fluorescent tubing in a look that imitated
Fritz Lang's cult film *Metropolis* (1927).

1993 Ravers at Fantazia, UK
Ravers at the Fantazia festival
in Wiltshire. Customized dungarees,
baggy sweatshirts, floppy hats
and rainbow-striped gloves indicate
the close relationship between Rave,
Indie and hippie style: anti-fashion that
in America would be called Grunge.

**1994 Kate Moss backstage
at a fashion show**
The fashion world's obsession with
thinness and the new trend in fashion
photography to feature emaciated
models in disturbing, sleazy settings
raised concerns about so-called 'Heroin
Chic' and its perceived glorification
of drug abuse. However, Western
fashion throughout the twentieth
century held thinness to be the ideal.

1993 Nirvana fan, Germany
Nirvana, Pearl Jam and Sonic Youth
were among the influential Grunge
indie bands rising to prominence in
the early 1990s whose followers mixed
thrift-store clothing with workwear
(checked lumberjack shirts and heavy
industrial boots), and a generally
slovenly appearance.

S/S 1993 Ensemble by Marc Jacobs for Perry Ellis

Jacobs' 1993 'Grunge' collection, inspired by the Seattle music scene, confirmed his position as the designer with unlimited streetcred and a loyal band of customers epitomizing cool, such as movie director and Hollywood royalty Sofia Coppola, but it resulted in his dismissal from Perry Ellis.

S/S 2009 Ensemble by Marc Jacobs

A grungy plaid vest-top edged with lurex is layered with metallic, striped skirts and a broad sash in a collection by Jacobs that combined his continuing love of edgy street style with turn-of-the-century Americana.

**2005 Gwen Stefani
and Harajuku Girls**
Japanese street style has been
disseminated in the West through
stars like Gwen Stefani, seen here
with her backing group, the Harajuku
Girls, whose dress is derived from
the Japanese school uniform, itself
derived from the nineteenth-century
Western sailor suit. In 2005 Stefani
launched her 'Harajuku Lovers'
clothing line.

2006 Harajuku Fruits
From the late 1970s until 2000
Harajuku's main drag was
pedestrianized, becoming a street
catwalk on which to perform and display:
so many and various are the looks born
out of Harajuku and other areas in Tokyo
and so rapid is the pace of change that
it is almost impossible to categorize
styles. The term *kawaii*, coined by *CUTiE*
magazine, is a general description:
prettiness, cuteness combined with
a daring, independent spirit, as worn
here by these 'Fruits'.

Designer: Minimal

'Modernity begins here, as a process of elimination: minimal seams, minimal weight, minimal care, minimal details. Minimalism is, I think, the future....'

Geoffrey Beene, interview with Grace Mirabella in *Geoffrey Beene Unbound* 1994

**Resort 2011 Dress
by Phoebe Philo for Céline**
Since becoming creative director at Céline, Phoebe Philo has merged urban cool with a rigorous aesthetic. Her recent collections have been hailed as some of the most important and potentially influential for several years.

1972 Dress by Jean Muir
At a time when most British designers were creating romantic fantasies, Jean Muir never wavered from her own classic, understated style, formed soon after she launched her label in 1966. Fluid Hurel jersey, butter-soft leather and suede in muted colours, especially dark navy, were given interest by the use of topstitching around seams.

1974 Lauren Hutton in Calvin Klein
Having cut his teeth on Seventh Avenue in the 1960s, New Yorker Calvin Klein became known for understated, elegant clothes in neutral colours and luxurious fabrics. Lauren Hutton wears a silk and cashmere cardigan, matching polo-shirt and trousers with jewellery by Bulgari.

1973 Utrasuede dress by Halston
Roy Halston, who trained as a milliner,
also specialized in 'poverty de luxe',
or expensive simplicity. His roster of glitzy
clients included Jackie Kennedy, whose
inauguration pillbox hat he designed.
In 1972 he launched a reinterpretation
of the classic shirtwaister: in washable,
crease-resistant Ultrasuede, it soon
became a classic in every New York
socialite's wardrobe.

S/S 1980 Pat Cleveland in Halston
Halston's flattering outfits were
popular on the drug-fuelled dancefloor
at Studio 54: an enthusiastic follower
of New York's hedonistic lifestyle during
the 1970s, he died in 1990, but the
label has since been revived under
the direction of Marios Schwab.

1983 Charlotte Rampling in Giorgio Armani

Actress Charlotte Rampling in Giorgio Armani's soft tailoring: from the late 1970s he applied his expertise in men's tailoring to women's outerwear, reducing structure to a minimum and using fluid fabrics such as light wools that caress the body. One of the largest privately owned global fashion brands, the Armani stable's numerous labels encompass all levels of fashion and lifestyle, from couture to underwear and chocolates.

1985 Azzedine Alaïa

Tunisian-born Alaïa invented second-skin dressing (including the original leotard/body in 1980, five years before Donna Karan) and became known as the 'King of Cling' for his empowering, body-con clothes in Lycra and leather, often adorned with studs and zippers.

**c. 1985 New York fashion,
American** *Vogue*
The little black dress is the ultimate
in minimalist dressing: here examples
by (L to R) Geoffrey Beene, Calvin Klein,
Oscar de la Renta and Jackie Rogers
demonstrate 1980s high-gloss glamour
for the evening.

1985 Dress by Marc Jacobs
A star-print dress teamed with opaque tights and flat ankle boots demonstrates Marc Jacobs' ability to transfer casual streetstyle to the catwalk. His career as head designer at Perry Ellis from 1988 ended when his notorious 1993 'Grunge' collection was considered too daring even for a label associated with youth and playfulness.

S/S 1997 Kate Moss in Marc Jacobs
Kate Moss in a sheer double-layered slip dress, as pared-down as possible, demonstrates Jacobs' increasing sophistication in the year he was taken on to revitalize the Louis Vuitton label, where he remains creative director.

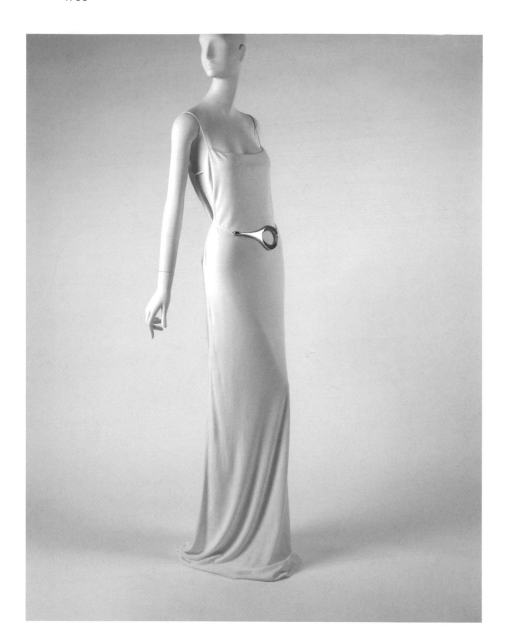

**1996/7 Evening dress
by Tom Ford for Gucci**
As glamorous as the Gucci label
he revitalized during the 1990s, Tom
Ford epitomizes the celebrity fashion
designer who attracts as much media
coverage as his clients. Inheriting
the mantle of American minimalism,
his pared-down yet sexy garments
frequently pay homage to the 1970s –
here a revealing white jersey dress
with gold fastenings.

**A/W 1999 Erin O'Connor
in Helmut Lang**
Austrian Helmut Lang's clothes achieved
cult status among fashion insiders during
the 1990s: they were sophisticated,
minimalist, sometimes futuristic, often
slightly disturbing and always ahead
of their time. This ensemble, which
includes an integral neck-rest, combines
leather and black organza. He gave
up the fashion business in 2005 and
now pursues a career as an artist.

S/S 2010 Trouser suit by Armani Privé
Armani's couture line, Armani Privé, is shown biannually in Paris and was the first to be streamed live on the internet, in 2007. For Spring/Summer 2010 his inspiration came from the moon: glimmering metallic fabrics cut with moon-shaped detailing were accessorized with crescent-shaped brooches.

A/W 2010 Dress by Calvin Klein
Market leader in designer denim, underwear and perfume for both sexes for a generation, Calvin Klein sold the company in 2003 for a colossal sum. Now headed up by Brazilian design director Francisco Costa, the brand remains a household name.

2010 Jacket by Jil Sander for Uniqlo
German designer Jil Sander's minimalism has set the bar for women's precision-cut tailoring in ultra-luxurious fabrics since the 1990s. Having left the company that bears her name, now under the direction of Raf Simons, she has collaborated with Japanese retailer Uniqlo, delivering high standards of manufacture to the high street.

Designer: Colour

'Look! Who says there are only colours?
There are also shades!'

Diana Vreeland on Missoni 1969

1975 Ensemble by Missoni
Since the late 1960s the Missoni family
has taken machine-knitting to new levels
of sophistication: their jazzy geometric
patterns, mixing up Art Deco ziggurats
with stripes in kaleidoscopic colour,
enlivened a previously conventional
craft. The artisanal approach of much
of Italy's manufacturing has resulted
in exceptionally close relationships
between designers and industry.

1975 Knitwear by Bill Gibb

The king of mix and match, Bill Gibb's multilayered knits, on which he collaborated with textile designer Kaffe Fassett, reflect the 1970s trend towards simplified kimono shapes. For the next decade knitwear surged in popularity.

A/W 1984 Kenzo

A plaid skirt and Fair-Isle-knit sweater worn over a Chinese floral top and trousers, with Peruvian shawl, hat and embroidered gauntlets demonstrate Kenzo Takada's genius for combining colour, print and pattern. In 1970 he was the first Japanese designer to show in Paris, where he opened his Jungle Jap boutique. His exuberant style breathed a joyful sense of fun into high fashion, but did not sell so well in the 1980s and '90s. The house has been revived under Antonio Marras, creative director since 1993.

1987 Evening gown
by Christian Lacroix

The unashamed luxury of Christian Lacroix's designs epitomized the 1980s. His use of intricate, labour-intensive trimming, combined with a taste for theatrical silhouettes (he originated the puffball skirt) often referenced his Provençal roots. An evening gown with sequinned bodice and 'front pouf' skirt demonstrate Lacroix's extrovert style and mastery of colour (it is hard to combine brown and black successfully). His couture house, founded in 1987, fell into financial difficulties in the new age of austerity and although it continues, he is no longer at the helm.

1991 Gianni Versace
and supermodels

One of the most successful in the fashion industry, the Versace brand was established in the late 1970s in Milan and became known for its blatant display of sexuality and wealth: revealing, brash and ostentatious. Yet Gianni Versace was a skilled cutter and experimental in his use of fabrics, traits that have continued to differentiate the label under the directorship of his sister Donatella, since his murder in 1997. Known for his links to pop musicians and film-stars, his shows featured the supermodels of the day, including Naomi Campbell here in a beaded jumpsuit.

**A/W RTW 1994 Ensemble
by Romeo Gigli**
Romeo Gigli showed his first collection
in 1983, bucking current trends by
introducing a soft, romantic look using
richly coloured velvets, embroidery,
brocades and silks that refer back
to historical styles and Orientalism.
He continues to show his collections
in Milan.

**S/S 1994 'Flying Saucer' dress
by Issey Miyake**
Issey Miyake's 'Flying Saucer' dress
combines vivid, convoluted bands
of colour with playful distortion of the
silhouette, a perennial theme in his
work. The shapes that fabric creates
on and with the body are also explored
through his 'Issey Pleats' (S/S 1989)
and 'Pleats Please' (S/S 1994) lines.

**A/W RTW 1997 Detail
of separates by Sonia Rykiel**
Known as 'The Queen of Knits',
Sonia Rykiel opened a boutique
on the Left Bank in Paris in 1968
selling contemporary, easy-to-wear
pieces in her signature black and
colourful stripes. Still a family business,
the label continues to combine an
innovative approach with the day-
to-day needs of modern women.

**S/S RTW 1998 'Homage
to Frida Kahlo' collection
by Jean Paul Gaultier**
Always referred to as the *'enfant terrible'*
of fashion, a cliché he has taken
years to live down, Jean Paul Gaultier
broke many barriers in fashion, such
as dressing men in skirts, transforming
underwear into outerwear and using
black models. Eclectic sources of
inspiration characterize his collections,
including an homage to Frida Kahlo,
whose colourful style, based on ethnic
Mexican dress, continues to be an
iconic fashion statement.

**A/W Couture 2005 Ensemble
by John Galliano for Dior**
Extravagant, theatrical, romantic,
nostalgic and decadent are just a few
of the words used to describe the work
of John Galliano, whose inspiration
was drawn from a myriad of ideas
garnered during historical research
and world travel. A self-assured
use of vibrant colour has been his
trademark, epitomized here in a
collection which fused Dior's New
Look with Peruvian High Andes style.

**A/W Couture 2009 Ensemble
by John Galliano for Dior**
Galliano's collections were always
themed, this one inspired by archive
photographs of Christian Dior preparing
for a show. The sedate colours of the
New Look were replaced by a palette
of violets, mauves, fuschias, acid-yellows
and animal prints, combined with visible
corsetry and underpinnings in midnight
blue, black and flesh tones.

**S/S RTW 2006 Ensemble
by Dries Van Noten**
The skilful juxtaposition of prints
and patterns inspired by ethnic textiles
has been Dries Van Noten's hallmark:
watery silk ikats, delicate batiks,
brocaded Chinese chrysanthemums,
Ottoman stripes, embroidery and African
wax resists. Subtle colour combinations
are occasionally punctuated by a shot
of gold or leopard-print. This focus
on pattern and colour, rather than cut,
sets him apart from the other members
of the so-called 'Antwerp Six' such
as Ann Demeulemeester, although
recent collections have featured more
utilitarian fabrics in muted tones.

A/W 2008 Mintdesigns
In a collection called 'Trash, Slush
and Flash!', quirky Japanese design
duo Mintdesigns mingled shredded
paper with printed graphics on plastic
coats, bold monochrome knitted
separates and trademark patterned
socks. Their experimental approach
encompasses many projects, from cake
decoration to conceptual street art.

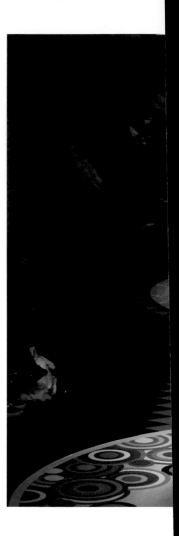

A/W 2008 Separates by Prada
Since taking over the family business in 1978, Miuccia Prada has used an intellectual approach to steer the house into its position as one of the most respected Italian fashion labels in the business. Her use of colour is unusual: beige and orange is a challenging combination, but in her search for novelty, she often sets out to question notions of good and bad taste.

S/S 2009 Coat by Manish Arora
Indian designer Manish Arora used the circus as inspiration for his wildly colourful collection: it may have had a Western theme, but it used all the technical skills of traditional handcrafts still practised in his native country. Having set up his label in 1997, he showed at Fashion Week in London and in Paris, gaining a reputation not just as India's premier designer, but as an international designer. In February 2011 he was appointed creative director of revived fashion house Paco Rabanne.

**S/S 2010 Dress
by Alexander McQueen**
Digital prints individually engineered for each sharply-cut garment in Alexander McQueen's 'Plato's Atlantis' collection, one of his most well recieved, were featured in a range of reptilian colours from turquoise to green and brown, worn with matching twelve-inch-high 'armadillo' shoes.

Designer: Concept

'What I have been trying to do, and what
I have probably done, is to make clothes that
seem to have existed for a long, long time.
In reality they never existed. I am not a
designer who creates fashionable aesthetics.
I make style out of life, not style out of style.'

Issey Miyake 1984

2010 132 5. ISSEY MIYAKE
Traditional Japanese clothing can
be laid flat, a characteristic that Issey
Miyake often explores. His '132 5.'
comprises computer-designed three-
dimensional shapes that become folded
polygons made from recycled plastic,
or PET, that are pulled up over the body
to form three-dimensional garments.

1982 Sweater and skirt by Rei Kawakubo for Comme des Garçons
Rei Kawakubo and Yohji Yamamoto showed separately in Paris for the first time in 1981. It turned out to be the biggest shake-up in fashion since Dior's New Look in 1947: 'Post-Hiroshima chic' and the 'bag lady look' soon became the fashion insider's uniform. Delight in irregularity and imperfection is part of the Japanese cultural aesthetic, referenced here in Kawakubo's deconstructed sweater with inbuilt holes, or 'lace'.

S/S 1983 Ensemble by Yohji Yamamoto
By their second Paris shows in 1982, Kawakubo and Yamamoto had proved that fashion could come from non-Western cultures. Yamamoto's white cotton cut-work three-piece expresses his design ethos: 'I think perfection is ugly... I want to see scars, failure, disorder, distortion.'

S/S 1985 ISSEY MIYAKE
advertisement, *The Face*
The space created between clothes
and the body is a key element in
Miyake's early investigations into
clothing design. Layered and wrapped
fabric holds far more fascination than
tight, figure-revealing clothes. For
Miyake, textiles are the launchpad
for his innovative work, such as 'A-POC'
(A Piece Of Cloth), a continuous
knitted tube from which the wearer
cuts garments with a pair of scissors.

S/S 1997 Dress by Rei Kawakubo
for Comme des Garçons
Kawakubo's 'Dress Becomes Body
Becomes Dress' or 'Lumps' collection
(as it was more popularly known), was
a sensation, if demanding to wear.
Designing clothes for women who want
to attract with their minds rather than
their bodies, since Comme des Garçons
was formed in 1973, she has challenged
and overturned accepted notions
of female beauty.

S/S 1997 Dress
by Maison Martin Margiela
Maison Martin Margiela, established
in Paris in 1988, became known for its
deconstructionist approach, oversized
garments, and for sending models
down the catwalk with obscured faces.
Often referencing the history of fashion
by producing replicas of garments,
the Maison also invokes the tools and
processes involved in creating couture,
as in this dress that mimics fabric
sections pinned on a dressmaker's
dummy, playing with notions of the
ideal versus the real and the lifeless
form versus the moving model.

c. 2000 Zipper top
by Maison Martin Margiela
Now retired from the house that bears
his name, Martin Margiela is ironically
the best known Belgian designer,
despite being the most enigmatic.
Rarely interviewed, he remained hidden
behind a team that was as anonymous
as the house's blank or numbered
labels, unsignposted shops in backstreet
locations and shows in unlikely, desolate
venues. The house frequently recycles
secondhand materials, such as these
zippers remodelled into a bodice.

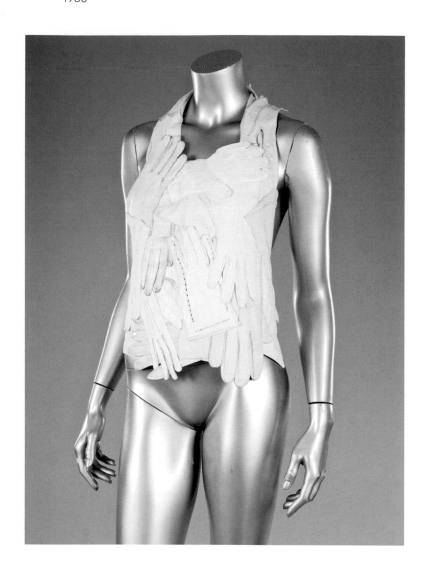

2001 Glove top
by Maison Martin Margiela
Interlocking white kid gloves formed
into a halter-neck bodice. These
'Artisanal' garments were expensive,
reflecting the labour-intensive nature
of the couture industry, but Margiela
was ahead of the times in highlighting
the need for sustainability.

A/W 2005 Ensemble
by Ann Demeulemeester
One of the so-called 'Antwerp Six'
who showed their work in London
in the late 1980s, Ann Demeulemeester
has earned a reputation for her
deconstructed tailoring (raw edges,
exposed seams) and for cutting the
best trousers in the industry. Her
androgynous look is softened by fur
and lace, but it is nearly always black.

Overleaf
S/S 2001 'Ventriloquy' collection
by Hussein Chalayan
To the sound of a live orchestra,
Chalayan's *Bladerunner*-styled models
performed against a backdrop of a
vanishing-point created by lines of LED
lights. At the end of the show, each
of three models smashed the sugarspun
glass clothes of her doppelgänger
with a hammer. A rigorously conceptual
designer, Chalayan has used LED
lighting in and on his clothes,
designed garments with aeronautically
engineered, mobile sections and clothes
that can be used as furniture or folded
into an envelope and airmailed.

S/S 1999 Alexander McQueen
Shalom Harlow as the Dying Swan, being spray-painted by robots borrowed from Fiat, at the climax of one of McQueen's most spectacular shows. Drawing inspiration from a myriad themes – from the British 'rape' of the Highlands (1995) to Charles Darwin and environmental pollution (2009), his collections were always controversial and sometimes disturbing. Accusations of mere showmanship were disproved by his ability to design carefully crafted clothes that sold.

A/W 2002/3 'Long Live the Immaterial' collection, Viktor & Rolf
Dutch design duo Viktor & Rolf embody the DNA of conceptual fashion: since their first couture collection in 1998 their designs have referenced countless wide-ranging and often surreal ideas from the atomic bomb to black holes. For the 'Long Live the Immaterial' collection they used bluescreen technology to project images of the urban and natural worlds onto their garments.

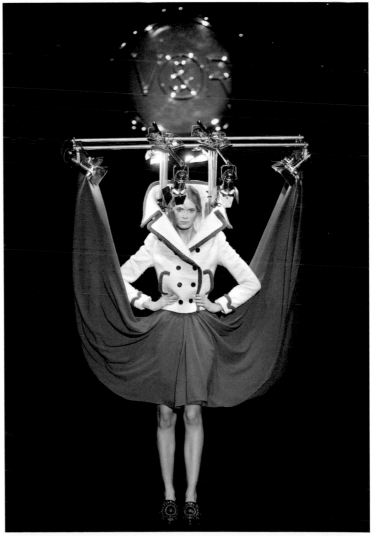

A/W 2007/8 Viktor & Rolf
In a collection inspired by Dutch
folklore, each outfit encapsulated
a stand-alone fashion show with its own
lighting and sound system, supported
by scaffolding. The performance artists
of the fashion world, Victor & Rolf
continue to design clothes that
are shown in sensational fashion.

A/W 2008/9 Jacket by Junya Watanabe for Comme des Garçons
Known as the 'techno couturier' Junya Watanabe has worked for Comme des Garçons since 1984 and shown his eponymous line in Paris under its umbrella since 1993. He is above all a brilliant fabric technician, whether folding crisp polyester into a multitude of honeycomb pleats or, as here, draping fluid fabrics around the body in a masterclass of manipulation, along the lines of Madeleine Vionnet.

A/W 2009/10 'Wonderland' collection by Rei Kawakubo for Comme des Garçons
Kawakubo's conceptually stimulating work, incorporating her clothes and the retail spaces designed by cutting-edge architects in which they are sold, continues to ensure that the Comme des Garçons label is one of the most watched and revered in fashion. Called 'Wonderland' by the designer, this collection featured blanket-coats and skirts layered with short utilitarian jackets, leggings, and flesh-coloured tulle draped over everything, including the faces of the models.

A/W 2010 Jacket and skirt by Yohji Yamamoto
Yamamoto's clothes are based on traditional Western formats, here a double-breasted jacket and pleated skirt, to which he brings a subtlety and restraint deeply rooted in Japanese culture. To him, black symbolizes the samurai spirit and like Kawakubo, who once declared that she 'designs in many shades of black', it remains the colour most associated with his work.

Designer: History and Heritage

'There is a way of living that has a certain grace and beauty. It is not a constant race for what is next, rather, an appreciation of what has come before.... There is a romance of living, a beauty in things that endure....'

Ralph Lauren on his Polo advertisements 1984

**A/W 2005/6 Erin O'Connor
in Couture John Galliano for Dior**
This collection evoked the spirit of Christian Dior, as had Galliano's debut collection for the house in 1997. Featuring garments inspired by a variety of nostalgic themes, from 'the mother of Christian Dior' to the New Look, it was both a hymn to couture and its processes and a demonstration of Galliano's febrile creativity.

S/S 1992 Jacket by Rifat Ozbek
Historical dress provided a rich seam
of inspiration for Ozbek: one of the
most iconic garments of 1992 was his
military-style jacket decorated with bone
beading recalling the hybrid Westernized
dress worn by North-American Indians
in the nineteenth century.

**S/S 1993 Ensemble
by Dolce & Gabbana**
Since the late 1980s, Italian design
duo Domenico Dolce and Stefano
Gabbana have consistently looked
back through history for inspiration,
whether that of their native country
and its cinema, or that of subcultural
dress, mixing it all up with humour and
irreverence. In 1993 they combined
Renaissance imagery with patchwork,
floppy hats and strings of beads
in a reprise of the hippie style.

**S/S 1996 Sack-back dress
by Vivienne Westwood**
Westwood's version of an eighteenth-
century sack-back dress, from
the collection 'Les Femmes', modelled
here by Linda Evangelista. Vivienne
Westwood continues to be one of the
most inspirational and creative fashion
designers of the age, applying her
intellectual approach and meticulous
historical research to collections
since the 1980s. Highly individual,
her clothes are empowering and sexy.

**S/S 1988 Separates
by Margaret Howell**
Margaret Howell began her career
making men's shirts in the 1970s
and has gone on to establish a British
brand that is one of the most respected
internationally. Quality fabrics and
workmanship give her clothes an integrity
that make them enduring classics.
On the beach in Sussex a white Irish-
linen shirt with lace collar is teamed
with wide-leg linen trousers and Doc
Martin lace-ups.

A/W 2009 Suit by Margaret Howell
An English worsted suit, pin-stripe cotton
and silk shirt, grey wool socks and flat
Oxfords epitomize Howell's modern
take on what is quintessentially British
menswear for women. Dufflecoats,
peacoats, mackintoshes, loafers
and saddlebags retail in her outlets
alongside vintage and contemporary
homewares with a modernist aesthetic.

A/W 1998 Eveningwear
by Paul Smith Women
Sir Paul Smith, who made his name in
menswear and is the most commercially
successful British designer today,
launched his women's range in 1994.
Quirky, original and playful, his ideas
are drawn from an eclectic range
of sources; a humourous, 'jumble sale'
approach that reinterprets vintage looks
with a modern sensibility, such as this
kitsch rose-print dressing-gown-style
evening dress.

S/S 2008 Separates
by Paul Smith Women
Early twentieth-century-style sports
blazer with striped rugger shirt
and pencil-slim trousers, worn by Lily
Cole with horn-rimmed round specs:
menswear for women injected with
humour and based on a deep
knowledge of tailoring.

2010 Ensembles
by Alexander McQueen
Jewel-bright fabrics encrusted with
Byzantine gems, sequins, rich gold
embroidery, and shimmering,
feathered angels' wings recalling
fifteenth-century altarpieces: the sixteen
outfits of McQueen's final collection
were lavishly decorated yet underpinned
by complex cutting and draping
on the stand by one of the world's
most original and fearless designers.

**A/W RTW 1991 Separates
by Karl Lagerfeld for CHANEL**
Karl Lagerfeld has achieved his greatest
fame by constantly updating the house
style and spirit of CHANEL, where
he has been head of design since
1983. Many of Mademoiselle's key
motifs can be seen here: the signature
tweed jacket, the silk bow tied at the
neck, the chain belt and the camellia in
Kristen McMenamy's hair. But Lagerfeld
has brightened the colour palette and
teamed classic pieces with a pair of
denim jeans, encrusted with gold *bijoux*.

**A/W RTW 2010 Suit
by Karl Lagerfeld for CHANEL**
After nearly thirty years at the helm,
Lagerfeld mixed up denim, leather,
tweeds and knits interwoven with fake
fur and glimmering silver, lengthening
the classic CHANEL cardigan jacket
into a peplum style worn with CHANEL's
signature two-tone footwear. The show
was staged as a winter wonderland,
complete with imported icebergs.

S/S 2010 Suit by Ralph Lauren
Ralph Lauren has made a phenomenally
successful career from delivering
versions of the imagined past: rose-
tinted nostalgia rooted in the collective
memory. From the prairies of the mid-
West to the hunting fields of Britain,
he has encapsulated all that is essential
and most appealing about any look:
here a 1930s-style suit complete with
stiff collared shirt, patterned tie and
newsboy cap gives a romantic gloss
to the Depression years.

S/S 2011 Ensemble by Ralph Lauren
Home on the range, Lauren showed
a gingham dress edged with lace,
a lace scarf, leather pants and bull's
head Western buckle in a collection
that mixed Victoriana with cowgirl chic.

**S/S 2010 Models backstage
at Burberry Prorsum**
From a functional gabardine trenchcoat
designed for soldiers during the First
World War, to glossy advertising
campaigns starring supermodels
and actors, Burberry has transformed
itself into an übercool brand under
the creative directorship of Christopher
Bailey, since 2001. The trenchcoat,
now available in a range of colours
and leather, sits alongside the globally
recognized check as an iconic symbol
of a British luxury brand, whose shows
under the media-savvy Bailey are
streamed live and in 3D across
the internet.

**2007 Victoria Beckham
with 'Birkin' bag**
The Hermès 'Birkin' bag (after
the actress Jane Birkin, for whom
it was originally designed) is highly
coveted, with waiting lists of up to
six years. According to press reports,
Victoria Beckham owns over 100
'Birkins', making her collection
worth £1.5 million.

2010 Shop display at Louis Vuitton
A leather goods and accessories brand, Louis Vuitton was founded in the mid nineteenth century and became synonymous with luxury, its monogram logo instantly recognizable the world over. Marc Jacobs' restrained ready-to-wear line for the label was outstripped by sell-out success in collaborations on handbags with artists such as Stephen Sprouse, who grafitti-ed the logo.

**A/W 1995 Kate Moss
in Tom Ford for Gucci**
Tom Ford was taken on by Gucci in
the late 1980s and was creative director
by 1994. The A/W 1995 collection,
a revival in velvet and satin of 1970s
glamour, was considered a triumph. Both
he and the brand enjoyed unparalleled
celebrity until his departure in 2004.

**A/W 2004 Outfit
by Tom Ford for Gucci**
The glamour that became synonymous
with the brand under Ford's direction is
epitomized here in fox fur and sunglasses
in a matching shade of magenta. After
leaving Gucci he launched a luxury
menswear line, but is perhaps better-
known for directing the film *A Single
Man* in 2009, set in a stylish 1960s
Los Angeles.

Pre Spring 2010 Ensemble by Nicolas Ghesquière for Balenciaga
Skinny pants teamed with shrunken tailoring on a 1970s-style appliquéd-leather jacket. Having trained with Jean Paul Gaultier, Nicolas Ghesquière was brought in to revive the house of Balenciaga in 1997, since when he has injected the 'Master's' signature architectural style with a modern sensibility that has made the label relevant once again.

A/W RTW 2009/10 Ensemble by Riccardo Tisci for Givenchy
Having dressed the world's most iconic women, from Jackie Kennedy to Maria Callas, Hubert de Givenchy retired from his eponymous label in 1995. At the helm John Galliano, Alexander McQueen and Julien Macdonald were followed by Riccardo Tisci, creative director since 2004, who has gained a reputation for craftsmanship and polish.

Fashion and Fame

'I so wanted to be like you in *Breakfast at Tiffany's* that I put my hair in two ponytails, bought huge sunglasses, and wore the closest thing to "you" I could put together. I got suspended from school for the sunglasses....'

Letter from Cher to Audrey Hepburn quoted in Barry Paris: *Audrey Hepburn* 1998

**1961 Audrey Hepburn
in *Breakfast at Tiffany's***
Audrey Hepburn redefined ideals of feminine beauty in the 1950s. Her slim, boyish figure and brunette features bucked the trend for blonde bombshells: she immediately became a fashion icon whose accessible look was copied by millions, even if only by donning a pair of huge sunglasses. For many of her screen roles, including Holly Golightly in *Breakfast at Tiffany's*, she was dressed by Givenchy: the long black evening dress she wears here, one of three made for the film, was sold at auction in 2006 for nearly half a million pounds.

1962 Brigitte Bardot
Brigitte Bardot's unconventional
lifestyle was mirrored by her
unconventional clothes: preferring jeans,
sloppy joes, simple gingham dresses
and bare feet, she was the antithesis
of what a film-star was supposed to look
like. With her tousled hair and smudgy
eye makeup, she more often looked
as if she had just got out of bed than
out of the dressing room.

**A/W RTW 1995 Kate Moss
in Karl Lagerfeld for CHANEL**
Moss styled in Bardot's image,
in a CHANEL cardigan that could have
come straight from the 1960s. Moss's
personal style off the catwalk is often
reminiscent of Bardot and also highly
influential. Moss traded in on her look
in a three-yeear collaboration with retail
entrepreneur Philip Green, owner
of Topshop, from 2007 to 2010.

**1961 'Jackie lookalikes'
in Oleg Cassini**
Jackie Kennedy shaped her own image
as the epitome of American chic. Though
she favoured couture from European
houses Givenchy and Balenciaga she
recognized the importance of supporting
American talent and appointed Oleg
Cassini as her official designer. 'Jackie
look' models pose in Cassini's neat suits
and Jackie's trademark pillbox hat.

**1965 Lee Radziwill and Jackie
Kennedy in London**
Throughout the 1960s Jackie and
her sister Lee Radziwill consistently
appeared on the World's Best-Dressed
List. At her first husband's funeral Jackie
was dressed in Givenchy; at her second
marriage, to Aristotle Onassis in 1968,
in Valentino; but her sartorial legacy
is defined by the style of sunglasses
she favoured. Baskets of huge, 'Jackie
O' styles were kept just inside
her front door.

**1983 Nancy Reagan
in James Galanos**
The 'Gilded Age' of the Reagan
presidencies was characterized by
lavish social functions, unashamed
displays of wealth and conspicuous
consumption. Nancy Reagan was
passionate about designer clothes,
filling twelve double closets at the
White House. Her favoured designers
included Bill Blass, Adolfo, Oscar
de la Renta and Californian James
Galanos, whose evening gown
she wears here.

**2011 Michelle Obama
in Alexander McQueen**
Michelle Obama has shown herself
to be fiercely independent in her
wardrobe choices, often choosing
lesser-known international labels
such as Junya Watanabe. She hosted
a dinner for China's premier in a
vivid blood-orange gown by Sarah
Burton for Alexander McQueen:
in response to criticism, she declared
that women should wear what
they want.

Previous spread
1981 Diana, Princess of Wales
Lady Diana Spencer's wedding gown,
designed by Elizabeth and David
Emanuel, was a fairytale confection
of taffeta and lace with a twenty-five-
foot train that created an unforgettable
image of the transition from gauche
Sloane Ranger to Princess. In her
new role she became the most
photographed woman in the world,
her fashion choices making headlines.

1995 Diana, Princess of Wales in Versace
Until the breakdown of her marriage and divorce in 1996, Diana, Princess of Wales, did much to promote London-based designers such as Catherine Walker, Bruce Oldfield and Christina Stambolian. She later became more international in her fashion choices: Versace, whose pale pink suit she wears here, was a favourite. She attended his funeral two months before her own death in 1997.

2011 Catherine Middleton arriving at Westminster Abbey
Catherine Middleton's wedding dress by Sarah Burton, now head designer at Alexander McQueen, was romantic and elegant. Ivory satin trimmed with handmade appliquéd lace was given a modern twist with house-style draping at the back. A tiara loaned by the Queen and simple bouquet containing Sweet William completed the enchanting spectacle.

1984 Madonna at the MTV Awards
Madonna's rise to mega-stardom ran in tandem with the success of MTV, launched in 1981. Through music videos played on the channel, pop-stars became far more visible. At the start of her career, Madonna wore an edgy, street look of lace, fishnets, tacky jewellery and bleached hair, as she did in the film *Desperately Seeking Susan* (1985).

1990 Madonna in Jean Paul Gaultier, 'Blond Ambition' tour
By the 1990s Madonna's performances and costumes on stage were breaking taboos, blending eroticism with Catholic imagery. For the 'Blond Ambition' tour she wore a pink satin corset with conical cups designed by Jean Paul Gaultier, who turned underwear into outerwear, an enduring theme in his work.

1985 Barbie and Ken in Jean Paul Gaultier
Celebrity comes in many shapes and sizes: since her birth (launch) in 1959, Barbie has been a star, charting the course of fashion and ideal beauty throughout her long career. Many designers have dressed her, including Jean Paul Gaultier, who teams a ruched chartreuse velvet corset-dress with conical 'bombshell' bra cups with a bobble hat, while her consort Ken wears a gender-bending skirt suit.

1952 Marilyn Monroe, USA

Original caption: 'The most torrid thing to hit Hollywood since the days of the first Blonde Bombshell Jean Harlow is the scintillating Marilyn Monroe. Whether she wears a potato sack [as here], a flimsy summer dress... or a plunging neck lined gown..., the sexy screen favorite radiates the same irresistible charm, something that borders on outright witchcraft.'

S/S 1992 Cindy Crawford in 'Sack' dress by Dolce & Gabbana

Domenico Dolce and Stefano Gabbana successfully combined forces to become one of the leading Italian brands by the early 1990s. Their 1992 S/S *La Dolce Vita* collection, based on Fellini's 1960 film, showcased a galaxy of supermodels on the catwalk – here Cindy Crawford in a dress emblazoned with provocative text, inspired by a photograph (left) of Marilyn Monroe wearing an outfit made from potato sacking.

1994 Elizabeth Hurley in Versace
No designer understood the value
of celebrity endorsement better than
Gianni Versace. When Liz Hurley
attended the premiere of the film *Four
Weddings and a Funeral* with her then
boyfriend Hugh Grant, Versace lent
her a show-stopping dress barely
fastened with golden safety pins
at each side and a plunging neckline.
It ensured Hurley's trajectory towards
celebrity and invaluable press
coverage for the designer.

2008 Miley Cyrus in Valentino
'Red carpet' dressing is now part
of the fashion calendar as award
ceremonies for music, film and television
give designers an opportunity to show
their most lavish gowns on a glittering
array of stars. Valentino is a favourite
choice, especially in his trademark
'Valentino red'.

2007 Actors in costume from *Mad Men*
Mad Men, the American cable-TV show launched in 2007, has won acclaim for its evocation of life in a 1960s New York advertising agency. Actors were picked for their natural looks, unenhanced by cosmetic treatment, while careful research led to authentic-looking costumes. Its cult success has led to spin-off merchandising including a Brooks Brothers suit, nail varnish and a website where avatars can be dressed in *Mad Men* style.

A/W 2010 Coat by Miuccia Prada
Miuccia Prada's 2010 A/W collection recalled 1960s style, from beehive hairdos to wingtip spectacles. Her signature scratchy grid prints appeared on simple A-line dresses and coats with slightly raised waistlines, emphasizing feminine curves.

**2007 Sarah Jessica Parker
in Vivienne Westwood, as Carrie
in *Sex and the City***
Sex and the City (launched 1998)
influenced a generation of young
women who copied the characters'
styles, wearing their own version
of the 'Carrie' necklace and lusting
after Manolo Blahnik's shoes. The show
was costumed by award-winning Patricia
Field, who now has her own clothing
company that mixes designer pieces
with street fashion. When Carrie
was left standing at the altar in
the first spin-off movie, she wore
a Vivienne Westwood bridal gown.

**2010 Lady Gaga
in Nicola Formichetti**
Assuming many different personas
and guises, Stefani Germanotta as Lady
Gaga has appeared on the red carpet
in outrageous costumes as well as
couture, from Armani Privé to Alexander
McQueen. Here at the Brit Awards she
wears a costume by Nicola Formichetti,
her stylist, who has recently been
appointed creative director of fashion
house Thierry Mugler. Gaga is tipped to
have a hand in forthcoming womenswear
collections for the revamped label.

Picture Credits

6 The Ernestine Carter Collection / The Fashion Museum, Bath & North East Somerset Council **10** Photo by Paul Boyer / Mansell / Time Life Pictures / Getty Images **12** Photo by General Photographic Agency / Getty Images **13 top** Photo by Eugene Robert Richee / Getty Images **13 bottom** Photo by the Olive Matthews Collection, Chertsey Museum / Photograph by John Chase **15** Courtesy of Maryhill Museum of Art **16** © Bettmann / Corbis **18 left** Photo by W. & D. Downey / Getty Images **18 right** Photo by Time Life Pictures / Mansell / Time Life Pictures / Getty Images **19** Photograph © The State Hermitage Museum / photo by Vladimir Terebenin, Leonard Kheifets, Yuri Molodkovets **20** The Museum and Study Collection, Central Saint Martin's College of Art and Design **21 left** National Trust Photographic Library / John Hammond / The Bridgeman Art Library **21 right** Hulton Archive / Getty Images **22** The Museum and Study Collection, Central Saint Martin's College of Art and Design **23** Fashion Museum, Bath and North East Somerset Council / The Bridgeman Art Library **24** © V&A Images **25** Photo by Popperfoto / Getty Images **26** Photo by Topical Press Agency / Getty Images **27** Private Collection **28** © Matthew Polak / Sygma / Corbis **29** Private Collection **30** The Art Archive / Kharbine-Tapabor **31** The Art Archive / Kharbine-Tapabor / Collection IM **32 left** © V&A Images **32 right** The Museum and Study Collection, Central Saint Martin's College of Art and Design **33** The Museum and Study Collection, Central Saint Martin's College of Art and Design **34** Photo by Branger / Roger Viollet / Getty Images **35** © The Philadelphia Museum of Art / Scala **36** Photo by Muriel Straithmore / Topical Press Agency / Getty Images **37** The Art Archive / Kharbine-Tapabor **38 left** Photo by Hulton Archive / Getty Images **38 right** Portrait of Rita de Acosta Lydig, 1911 (oil on canvas), Boldini, Giovanni (1842–1931) / Private Collection / Photo © Christie's Images / The Bridgeman Art Library **39 top and bottom** © The Metropolitan Museum of Art / Art Resource New York / Scala, Florence **40** © The Gallery Collection / Corbis **41** The Advertising Archives **42** Photo by Imagno / Getty Images **44** The Museum and Study Collection, Central Saint Martins College of Art and Design **45** Photo by Transcendental Graphics / Getty Images **46** © V&A Images **47** Photo by Hulton Archive / Getty Images **48 left and right** Photo by Imagno / Getty Images **49** Photo by Imagno / Getty Images **50 left** The Tate Archive **50 right** University of Leeds Art Collection, Gift of Stanley Burton, 1965 **51** Photo by Hulton Archive / Getty Images **52–53** The Art Archive / Kharbine-Tapabor **54** Collection of the Kyoto Costume Institute, photo by Takashi Hatakeyama **55** Photo by Hulton Archive / Getty Images **56** Photo by Henri Manuel (Apic / Getty Images) **57** The Museum and Study Collection, Central Saint Martin's College of Art and Design **58** The Art Archive / Kharbine-Tapabor / Collection IM **59** Photo by Lipnitzki / Roger Viollet / Getty Images **60** © Mary Evans Picture Library 2008 **61** © V&A Images **62** Courtesy Elisabeeta Seeber **63** The Kobal Collection / Istituto Luce **64** © Photo Scala, Florence **65** Private Collection **66** © Oliver Krato dpa / lnw **67** © V&A Imuges **68** © Museum of London **70** © Bettmann / Corbis **71** © Museum of the City of New York, USA / The Bridgeman Art Library **72–73** Fashion Museum, Bath and North East Somerset Council / The Bridgeman Art Library **74 left** The Art Archive / Kharbine-Tapabor **74 right** © Clifton R. Adams / National Geographic Society / Corbis **75** Photo by Topical Press Agency / Getty Images **76 top** Imperial War Museum **76 bottom** Imperial War Museum **77 top** Photo by FPG / Hulton Archive / Getty Images **77 bottom** © Corbis **78 top** The Art Archive / Kharbine-Tapabor **78 bottom** Photo by Topical Press Agency / Getty Images **79** Private Collection **80** © DaZo Vintage Stock Photos / Images.com / Corbis **81** © Mary Evans Picture Library 2010 **82** The Advertising Archives **83** © the Olive Matthews Collection, Chertsey Museum / Photograph by John Chase **84** © the Olive Matthews Collection, Chertsey Museum / Photograph by John Chase **85** Photo by Keystone / Getty Images **86–87** Private Collection **88** © Hulton-Deutsch Collection / Corbis **90** Photo by SSPL / Getty Images **91 top** Photo by Hulton Archive / Getty Images **91 bottom** Photo by H F Davis / Getty Images **92** Photo by Topical Press Agency / Getty Images **93** The Stapleton Collection **94** Photo by Imagno / Getty Images **95** Photo by SSPL / Getty Images **97** Private Collection **98** © V&A Images **99** © ullsteinbild / TopFoto **100** © Bettmann / Corbis **101** Private Collection **102** © Condé Nast Archive / Corbis **103** Photo by Archive Photos / Getty Images **104** Private Collection **105** © Bettmann / Corbis **106** Photo by Bob Thomas / Popperfoto / Getty Images **107** © Corbis **108** Private Collection **109** Photo by Kirby / Hulton Archive / Getty Images **110** © Julio Donoso / Sygma / Corbis **112** The Stapleton Collection **113** Photo Roger Viollet / Getty Images **114** © the Olive Matthews Collection, Chertsey Museum / Photograph by John Chase **115** © The Metropolitan Museum of Art / Art Resource / Scala, Florence **116** Photo by Apic / Getty Images **117** © Condé Nast Archive / Corbis **118** Victoria & Albert Museum, London, UK / The Bridgeman Art Library **119** © The Metropolitan Museum of Art / Art Resource / Scala, Florence **120** Private Collection **121** © The Metropolitan Museum of Art / Art Resource / Scala, Forence **122** Photo by Time Life Pictures / Pictures Inc. / Time Life Pictures / Getty Images **123** © V&A Images **124** Courtesy CHANEL / © Man Ray Trust / ADAGP Paris 2011 **125 left** Courtesy of Verdura Inc **125 right** Photo by Michael Ochs Archives / Getty Images **126** © V&A Images **127** © Condé Nast Archive / Corbis **128** © Condé Nast Archive / Corbis **129** © Philadelphia Museum of Art / Corbis **130** © Art Resource, New York Scala, Florence **131** © Mary Evans Picture Library 2010 **132** Photo by Eugene Robert Richee / John Kobal Foundation / Getty Images **134** Photo by Ira L. Hill / FPG / Getty Images **135 left** Photo by Popperfoto / Getty Images **135 right** Kjeld Duits Collection / MeijiShowa.com **136** © Underwood & Underwood / Corbis **137** Keystone / Hulton Archive / Getty Images **138** © The Olive Matthews Collection, Chertsey Museum / Photograph by John Chase **139** © the Olive Matthews Collection, Chertsey Museum / Photograph by John Chase **140** Photo by George Hurrell / John Kobal Foundation / Getty Images **141** The Advertising Archives **142** Photo by George Hurrell / John Kobal Foundation / Getty Images **143** Private Collection **144** © Bettmann / Corbis **145** Photo by Eugene Robert Richee / John Kobal Foundation / Getty Images **146** Photo by Hulton Archive / Getty Images **147** Private Collection **148** © Mary Evans Picture Library 2010 **150** © Corbis **151** Photo: akg-images **152** Private Collection **153** Photo by Kurt Hutton / Hulton Archive / Getty Images **154** The Advertising Archives **155** Photo by Galerie Bilderwelt / Getty Images **156** © Albert Harlingue / Roger-Viollet / Topfoto **157** The Art Archive / Kharbine-Tapabor / Collection Gantier **158** The Art Archive / Kharbine-Tapabor **159** Photo by Ralph Morse / Time Life Pictures / Getty Images **160** Photo by Fred Ramage / Hulton Archive / Getty Images **161** The Art Archive / Kharbine-Tapabor **162** Photo by Popperfoto / Getty Images **163** Photo by Fred Ramage / Hulton Archive / Getty Images **164** © V&A Images **165** © the Olive Matthews Collection, Chertsey Museum / Photograph by John Chase **166 left** Photo by Hulton Archive / Getty Images **166 right** Photo by Popperfoto / Getty Images **167** © Howell Walker / National Geographic Society / Corbis **168** The Advertising Archives **169** Photo by Fred Ramage / Hulton Archive / Getty Images **170** Photo by A R Tanner / Getty Images **171** Museo Salvatore Ferragamo **172** Courtesy of Maryhill Museum of Art **173** Courtesy of Pati Palmer from 'Théâtre de la Mode: Fashion Dolls – The Survival of Haute Couture', Palmer / Pletsch Publishing, Portland, Or. **174** Photo by Pat English / Time Life Pictures / Getty Images **176** © V&A Images **177** © The Metropolitan Museum of Art / Art Resource / Scala, Florence **178** © Bettmann / Corbis **179** Private Collection **180** © Condé Nast Archive / Corbis **181** © V&A Images **182** Photo by Loomis Dean / Time Life Pictures / Getty Images **183** Courtesy of Kerry Taylor Auctions **184** © Mary Evans

Index

Acknowledgements

For Glen

The scope of this book has at times been a daunting prospect; I am indebted to many people for helping me to bring it to fruition.

Thanks to the team at Laurence King, especially Laurence for his boundless enthusiasm, also Helen Rochester and Melissa Danny who have been models of consideration and patience. Heather Vickers' cheerful support and persistence as picture researcher has been invaluable as ever, as was Jennifer Jeffries' help in the initial stages. David Tanguy and the team at Praline have made it look beautifully elegant.

Grateful thanks to Rosemary Harden, Elaine Uttley and Vivien Hynes at The Fashion Museum, Bath; Grace Evans, Valerie Cumming and Veronica Isaac at Chertsey Museum; Rie Nii at The Kyoto Costume Institute; Deirdre Murphy at Kensington Palace; Beatrice Behlen at The Museum of London; Martin Pel at Brighton Museum; Layla Bloom at University of Leeds Art Collection; Marie Hamelin at Conservatoire Chanel; Francesca Piani at Museo Salvatore Ferragamo; Betty Long-Schleif at Maryhill Museum; Patti Palmer at Palmer/ Pletsch Publishing; Elisabetta Seeber; Kerry Taylor and Kate Mitchell at Kerry Taylor Auctions; Philip and Liz Debay at The Stapleton Collection; Emily Barneby at Harry Fane; Elizabeth Finkelstein; Will Whipple and From Somewhere; Andrew Macpherson; Donna Dumari; Venetia Scott; Richard Craig and Margaret Howell; Noel B. Chapman; Rose and Tony Hepworth; Mary Grimsditch, Jackson Trinder, Bonnie and Ophelia Blackman.

The support and encouragement of all my family and friends is invaluable: this book is for them, with my heartfelt thanks. I would also like to dedicate it to my inspirational alma mater, Central Saint Martin's College of Art and Design, where first and foremost I am grateful to Alistair O'Neill, Senior Research Fellow and course leader of Fashion History & Theory, whose generosity and friendship makes working with him such a pleasure. Thanks also to Judy Lindsay at the CSM Museum & Archive, Professor Caroline Evans, Professor Louise Wilson, Hywel Davies, Steve Hill and the many other colleagues and students who make it what it is.

Superficially, fashion is about image and images that evoke emotional responses: choosing these images and categorizing them is a subjective business and bound to be contentious, but I hope my selection will excite, intrigue, amuse and interest anyone who is seduced by fashion and that is, after all, as Oscar Wilde said, most of us.